There is no mystery like prayer. *The Sacred Echo* honors the mystery, and offers wise council along the way.

JOHN ORTBERG
Author and pastor,
Menlo Park Presbyterian Church

⁓

Margaret Feinberg's *The Sacred Echo* will stir you to approach prayer in a fresh and deeper way.

CRAIG GROESCHEL
Author of *It* and Senior Pastor,
LifeChurch.tv

⁓

When we feel like giving up on our prayers and begin doubting if they are making any difference, Margaret guides us back into hope and truth. *The Sacred Echo* not only reminds us of our need to never give up praying, but how God is wrapped up in every word we ever present to him.

DAN KIMBALL
Author of *They Like Jesus
but Not the Church*

⁓

Margaret Feinberg's words are a balm. As you read, you cannot help but sense that you are desperately loved. When we finally understand that, everything else gets a little easier. The burdens get a little lighter. And the world seems to get a little nicer.

SHANE CLAIBORNE
Author, activist, and recovering sinner
www.thesimpleway.org

Pay very close attention to words of my friend Margaret. Her wisdom and unique insight on connecting with our Maker is truly remarkable. Her words are prophetic. *The Sacred Echo* opened a new path for me to connect deeply with God in prayer.

MIKE FOSTER
President of Ethur and
founder of XXXchurch

Margaret Feinberg's *The Sacred Echo* gave me a new perspective on prayer. Very well written and thought-provoking, it helped me see prayer in a fresh light. Simply a must-read if your prayer life is stuck or in a rut.

DR. GARY SMALLEY
Author of *Change Your Heart,
Change Your Life*

This book should become a classic—but I hope not a classic more revered than enjoyed.

LEONARD SWEET
Drew University,
George Fox University,
www.sermons.com

Once again Margaret inspires her readers that the God of the universe wants to be "up close and personal" with his children, and his *Sacred Echo* is his relentless loving whisper to capture our hearts.

TAMMY DUNAHOO
Director of Foursquare Women,
National Church Office,
The Foursquare Church

Margaret is the real thing! Instead of writing on prayer with platitudes that reek of unrealistic piety and leave you feeling spiritually inept, Margaret's stories and winsome yet familiar-feeling encounters with God actually help you hear God's voice echo in your own soul.

DAVE TERPSTRA
Teaching Pastor,
The Next Level Church,
Denver

This really isn't a book just about prayer, but a book about a journey that leads to a deeper understanding of ourselves and a more surrendered life to the Echo of a God that is crazy in love with us. A must-read for anyone who is serious about their journey of faith and God's dream for their life.

JOHN BISHOP
Sr. Pastor, Living Hope Church

With deep insight into the narrative of prayer in Scripture, Margaret opens her life and invites us to follow her journey of holy conversations with God. Her authentic vulnerability has opened my eyes to new islands I want to explore to expand my relationship to the Trinity. This will be a book you won't be able to keep to yourself.

JOSH LOVELESS
STATUSpastor, discoveryCHURCH

Margaret Feinberg has done it again! Taking a well-versed subject, she has given it freshness and created a book that is personal, practical, and full of life.

AARON STERN
theMILL, new life church

In *The Sacred Echo*, Margaret gets real, and her stories, metaphors, and honesty encourage the reader to listen more closely to God as his voice reverberates through our life experiences like the beat of a familiar song.

AMENA BROWN
Poet and speaker

I really like the way Margaret tells stories about God. She makes them come to life!

JOSIE KIRK, 8
Reader in Olympia, Washington

Since the first printing of this book, readers have been making handwritten notes in the front of the book of the things they've learned about God. Then, they share the book with someone else. So we wanted to invite you to join the conversation. And while you're at it, we'd love to know: What are some of the sacred echoes in your heart?

the Sacred echo

Hearing God's Voice in Every Area of Your Life

margaret feinberg

ZONDERVAN®

ZONDERVAN.com/
AUTHORTRACKER
follow your favorite authors

We want to hear from you. Please send your comments about this book to us in care of zreview@zondervan.com. Thank you.

ZONDERVAN®

The Sacred Echo
Copyright © 2008 by Margaret Feinberg

This title is also available in a Zondervan audio edition. Visit www.zondervan.fm.

Requests for information should be addressed to:

Zondervan, Grand Rapids, Michigan 49530

Library of Congress Cataloging-in-Publication Data

Feinberg, Margaret, 1976 –
    The sacred echo / Margaret Feinberg.
        p.   cm.
    ISBN 978-0-310-27417-9 (hardcover)
      1. Spirituality. 2. Listening – Religious aspects – Christianity. 3. Christian life.
I. Title.
BV4501.3.F465   2008
248.4 – dc22   2008016851

Scripture taken from the *New American Standard Bible*. Copyright © 1960, 1962, 1963, 1968, 1971, 1972, 1973, 1975, 1977 by The Lockman Foundation. Used by permission.

Scripture quotations marked NIV are taken from the *Holy Bible, New International Version®*. NIV®. Copyright © 1973, 1978, 1984 by International Bible Society. Used by permission of Zondervan. All rights reserved.

Internet addresses (websites, blogs, etc.) and telephone numbers printed in this book are offered as a resource to you. These are not intended in any way to be or imply an endorsement on the part of Zondervan, nor do we vouch for the content of these sites and numbers for the life of this book.

Published in association with Yates & Yates, www.yates2.com.

Interior design by Beth Shagene

Printed in the United States of America

08 09 10 11 12 13 • 22 21 20 19 18 17 16 15 14 13 12 11 10 9 8 7 6 5 4 3 2 1

contents

foreword

There are some people who are so genuine and so nice that you can't not like them. Margaret Feinberg is one of them. Her warmth and authenticity seep through the pages of her books. By the time you turn the last page, you will feel like you've made a new friend.

I first discovered Margaret through her book *God Whispers: Hearing the Voice of God*, and over the years I've come to appreciate Margaret as an author, speaker, and friend. We only have a few guest speakers teach at National Community Church every year. Margaret is one of them. And every time she speaks, she not only challenges the way I think, but her intimacy with God inspires a deeper hunger to know God more.

In her latest book, *The Sacred Echo*, Margaret describes listening for God's voice not just as a whisper, but as an echo. She is convinced that when we listen for the sacred echoes —God's persistent voice—in our lives, then we can walk more confidently and fully into all that he has for us. Drawing on the story of Elijah on the mountainside, Margaret invites readers to open their eyes, ears, and hearts to what God is echoing in their lives. Using Scripture not only as a foundation but as the filter for all that we hear, she openly shares some of the echoes she's heard in her life. I'm confident they will resonate with some of the echoes you've heard in your own.

One of Margaret's unique gifts is the ability to put words to the subconscious fears and frustrations all of us experience. She opens up her heart and prayer life in a strikingly honest way. What I appreciate most is that she doesn't just share the answered prayers. She shares the unanswered prayers as well. Through it all, it's clear that her faith remains strong and her love for Jesus remains passionate.

Margaret is also not afraid to take her fears, doubts, and lack of faith before God and candidly ask, "What do I do with this?" In those moments, faith fuses with human experience and invites us to get a glimpse of life from a different perspective. In those moments, it's as if she discovers things about God she could not discover any other way. In the process, we all benefit as we gain glimpses into God's character, beauty, and mystery.

I also think you'll appreciate Margaret's unique spiritual insight. In one of my favorite chapters, *Read It Again*, I was challenged to not just read the Bible but really try to hear the voice of God. Margaret's ability to make lofty theological concepts and obscure biblical stories come alive is a rare gift, inspiring me to dive deeper into Scripture.

The Sacred Echo is a book about prayer. It's a book about hearing God's voice. It's a book about pursuing God. It's a book about all these things and so much more.

I pray that this book will be a milestone in your spiritual journey. May it rejuvenate your prayer life. And I hope you enjoy reading it as much as I did.

Mark Batterson
Lead Pastor
National Community Church
Washington D.C.

exposed

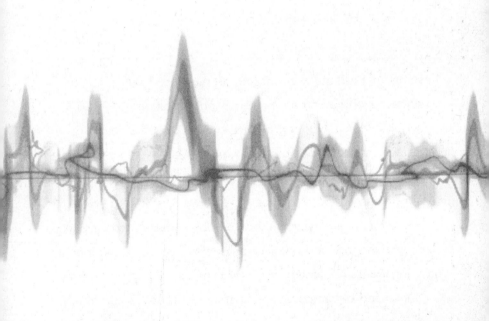

I'm not much of a pray-er. Well, maybe that's not quite ac-
curate. My mom, like most moms, would say I'm an answer to
her prayers—after years of infertility—but as far as being one
who prays, I probably leave something to be desired. I like
to pray, really, I do, but if left to my own devices, most of my
prayers sound a lot like scribbled grocery lists: random, disor-
ganized, and filled with less-than-healthy selections.

A few years ago, under the conviction that I needed to do
something about my crumpled, oft misplaced prayer life, I
started a journal. When the dainty notebook disappeared
under a chalky layer of gray dust behind the bed, so did my
resolve. I discovered both a few months later. With renewed
verve, I began studying contemplative prayer, centering
prayer, and Scripture prayer. I tried praying standing up,
sitting down, and lying on the floor. I committed to praying
early in the morning before work, unless I slept in, and late at
night, unless I dozed off. At one point, I started a photo prayer
journal and began collecting snapshots of friends and family
members in a shoebox. Those photos are still in a small card-
board box with leftover scrapbooking materials I have been
meaning to get to for, well, years now. Without realizing it, I
was becoming a yo-yo pray-er.

Then I had another idea. I'm still not sure where the lightbulb moment came from or how I can get another, but I decided to ditch the prayer journals altogether and develop a much simpler method. I created a prayer list in the back of my Bible on one of those blank, crispy-thin white sheets that serve as the extras in any Scripture binding. That way I couldn't easily misplace the list. Okay, technically I still could, but generally I lose my keys, sunglasses, and wallet—even my car in the parking lot of Costco—long before I ever lose my Bible. That's not to say it couldn't happen, but for over ten years, I've managed to carry the same well-worn, leather volume.

Now to write in your Bible is a serious thing, but to write prayers with the permanence of ink symbolized commitment not just to God but also to the people involved. I began my list slowly, selectively. Immediate family. Specific friends. Over the course of several weeks, names came to mind and stubbornly refused to leave. I carefully recorded each name, double-checking the spelling, using a black pen for consistency.

That was several years ago. Today, the list boasts different shades of blue, a flower-like doodle, and several coffee-colored stains and includes friends and nemeses, hopes and dreams, organizations and nations. Prayers and petitions, adoration and repentance, line the page. Like my grocery list, it's still a bit random to the casual observer, but through my conversations with God, prayer comes alive with a rhythm all its own.

Though prayer is much more than asking God for things, this single page in the back of my Bible remains a stark portrait of my faith.

Anyone can believe in God, perform the ritualistic rat-a-tat-tat of giving mental assertion, and even modify their behavior in response to a belief system, but prayers of petition force one to live eyes wide open to see what God may do or leave undone. I didn't realize that fateful day when I decided to turn my scribbled thoughts into a permanent list that I was accepting the invitation to not only ask God specific things but also to listen and watch for the answer—if one was given at all.

When I run my finger down the page, I realize most of my petitions haven't changed for years.

> Bless.
> Protect.
> Redeem.
> Heal.
> Restore.
> Reconcile.
> Renew.
> Guide.

Such requests are embarrassingly simple, yet God has listened to every one. As I reflect on this list—which is beginning to look war-torn over the years—I find myself marveling at the wonder of it all. God knows more about the people on the list than I ever will, and he loves them more deeply. He knows my prayers before they even leave my lips. If the God of the universe already knows everything before it happens, why do I bother praying, let alone engage in persistent prayer? Why keep tugging on God's sleeve day after day, month after month, year after year, with the same raggedy list of requests?

While struggling with these kinds of questions, I can't help but think of Jesus' parable of the tenacious widow who demanded justice. Though the local judge was a man without conscience ruling on matters however he saw fit, he finally caved and granted the woman's request. Why? Not because of the wisdom of her arguments, the eloquence of her speech, or the testimony of witnesses. He gave in simply because she was a nag and wore him down.

Interestingly, *nudnik* is the Yiddish word used by some Jewish translators to describe the bothersome widow. As a child, I often hovered behind my Jewish grandmother as she cooked, hoping for a scrumptious treat like a misshapen matzo ball or potato latke. She'd look at me sternly and say, "Stop being a *nudnik*!" Fortunately, I knew the secret every Jewish grandchild knows: If you pester long enough, your efforts will be rewarded.

Jesus uses the parable to make the case that if an unkind judge grants justice because of a nagging widow, how much more will God grant justice to his own children who cry out to him day after day?

Though I am grateful that he gives ear to those who have the tenacity to ask and keep on asking, I can't help but wonder:

Why?

Why pray a prayer a hundred times when God knew my heart's desire before the words left my lips the first time? Why cry out for justice repeatedly when God knows the depths of need more than I ever will? Why echo a prayer when God has already heard it countless times before? Though the *nudnik* woman was granted her request, how many others are denied every day—despite their persistence and perseverance? Why does prayer have to be so mysterious?

More than anything, I want to pray with the confidence that God will not only hear my words but act on them, and I want to listen with the confidence that when God speaks, I will recognize his voice and readily obey. I want a relationship with God where prayer is as natural as breathing. If God is the one in whom we are to live and move and have our being, then

I want my every inhale infused with his presence, my every exhale an extension of his love.

Yet even after a morning of focused prayer and study, an afternoon of life-changing conversation, or an evening listening to soul-stirring worship and teaching, I often find myself wondering: *God, was that really you? Was that your presence or my emotions? Was that your voice or my own?*

With so much unsure footing, I've been foraging the Scriptures for answers. I keep coming back to a familiar story of God's voice in the life of the prophet Elijah. Called to take on the false gods and unrighteous leaders of his day, Elijah finds himself on the run, a burned out, exhausted prophet who wants to give up. In 1 Kings 19, Elijah hits rock bottom and is ready to throw in the towel. God asks Elijah a simple but profound question: "What are you doing here, Elijah?" (v. 9).

Elijah's prophetic nature reminds him that God isn't a fan of phonies. He doesn't hold back: "I have been very zealous for the Lord, the God of hosts; for the sons of Israel have forsaken Your covenant, torn down Your altars and killed Your prophets with the sword. And I alone am left; and they seek my life, to take it away."

The prophet's life is on the line, yet God doesn't answer one of his concerns. For a hiccup of a moment, this passage makes me feel better about myself. I am not the only one whose laundry list of prayers seems to go unanswered.

Then God instructs Elijah to do something unusual: go stand on the side of a mountain and wait. I can only imagine the internal conversation Elijah was having with himself about God and the entire situation as he huffed across the rocky edge.

Standing thousands of feet above sea level, Elijah feels the wind pick up. Before he realizes what is happening, hurricane-force winds rip apart rock formations all around him. Then without warning, the wind calms. Next Elijah feels a rumbling under his feet. The prophet recognizes the unmistakable sounds of an earthquake. When the shaking finally stops, Elijah looks around skittishly. What's next?

That's when he sees the flames coming toward the mountain. Fire erupts all around, smoke filling the air. Elijah tries to buffer his face and mouth. Before he fully comprehends what's going on, the flames and smoke vanish, and Elijah experiences what he has been waiting for: God finally draws near to the worn-out prophet—in the quiet, gentle sound of a whisper.

Throughout this passage, we're reminded:

The Lord was not in the wind.

The Lord was not in the earthquake.

The Lord was not in the fire.

Yet God used a chain of natural—no, *supernatural*—events to prepare Elijah for an encounter with himself. The repeated display of power in the wind, earthquake, and fire didn't just get Elijah's attention—it also kept it.

God addresses the prophet, "What are you doing here, Elijah?"

Elijah offers a familiar answer, but this time God responds differently. He provides Elijah with specific instruction, encouragement, and even companionship. Our outrageously generous God provides for this torn-up prophet physically with food, emotionally with friendship, relationally with a wingman, Elisha, and spiritually with encouragement. God whispers life back into the prophet.

This story has always reminded me of just how much I need to be able to recognize God's whispers—those moments when he draws near and breathes words of life into my soul.

As I've continued to reflect on this passage, I've begun seeing something new that has been slowly transforming my prayer life and relationship with God. Namely, neither the wind, earthquake, or fire happened apart from God's knowledge or permission. In fact, God used these repeated demonstrations to prepare Elijah for an encounter with himself. And like an echo, God often uses the repetitive events and themes in daily life to get my attention and draw me closer to himself.

Now instead of just listening for God's whisper, I am trying to recognize the sacred echoes—those moments when God speaks the same message to my heart again and again. I call them *sacred echoes* because I've noticed that throughout my relationships, daily life, and study, the same scripturally sound idea or phrase or word will keep reappearing until I can no longer avoid its presence. Is this mere coincidence or is there something more?

When it comes to hearing from God, I firmly believe the Bible is our source and authority. God's Word is like a megaphone to his people. We recognize his voice best when we spend time listening to what he has to say through Scripture on a daily basis. Not only is God's Word the primary source of hearing from God, it is also our standard for filtering through the countless messages that bombard our minds and hearts each day. I love the description Paul gives to the Berean Jews: "They received the word with great eagerness, examining the Scriptures daily to see whether these things were so."

Though God's Word is our only source of indisputable truth, I cannot skip by the many passages of the Bible that illustrate how God speaks to his people. Throughout Scripture God speaks through kings and queens, princes and prophets, poets and pilgrims. He speaks through weather patterns, barnyard animals, and even the stars in the sky. God is not only creative, but he is persistent in getting our attention and communicating with us.

As I grow in my relationship with God, I find that he often uses the repetition of a phrase or word or idea represented in Scripture not only to get, but also to keep my attention. Like the persistent widow, God is a *nudnik* of sorts when it comes to drawing me back to himself. And I'm grateful. While a single whisper usually leaves me unsure, the repetitive nature of a sacred echo gives me confidence that God really is prompting, guiding, or leading. The sacred echo reminds me to pay close attention; something important may be going on here. The sacred echo challenges me to prayerfully consider how God is at work in my own life as well as the lives of those around me. The sacred echo is an invitation to spiritual awakening.

More and more, I'm finding that I need the sacred echo—the persistent voice of God—almost as if my life depended on it. The sacred echo reminds me he has not departed, he is steadfast, and he has not given up on me. If truth be told, as I grow older, I'm finding I need more certainty—not less—in responding to God's prompting in my life. Faith is not just moving forward when God seems far off. Faith is sometimes waiting until he is near to take the first step.

I am now taking one of those steps. I am about to share some of my most intimate prayers with you, those people and places and things I pray for steadily, sometimes with no reply, as well as those tender words I hear God echoing in my life time and time again. To be completely honest, sharing these things scares me. The fear isn't so much that you'll think I'm crazy, because at some point, I am confident you will.

My real fear is in being laid bare. Prayer is the place where I'm invited to present the parts of myself that no one else sees to a God who already knows and loves me anyway. You see, for me, my relationship with God is one of the most personal things I have. The tenderness of his presence. The longing to linger with him. The love that grips my heart and won't let go. I am in love—that I won't deny. As in any serious love affair, some things are meant to be kept just between the two of you. The problem is that for months now I've been sensing this consistent nudge to share what I'm discovering about God. This holy prodding has become so loud and clear through conversations, sermons, and books that even my husband, Leif, can hear it. Though I feel like I'm walking in obedience, I still can't shake the fear of transparency, because the words God speaks to my heart expose me like no other. In his love, God doesn't allow me to hide behind a handful of hastily plucked fig leaves. He wants to bring everything into the light.

Most of the prayers found in the upcoming pages center around my steady petitions and the toughest questions I ask God. There are many other aspects of prayer to explore—and I pray that you will. I know that I have a long way to go and grow in my understanding of God, but at the moment this is where I am. This is where I've been. This is also how far I still have to go.

You're about to discover some of the sacred echoes—the persistent voice of God—in my life. Through them I expect that the Spirit will further illuminate his presence in your life. You will hear his voice. You will feel his gentle prodding. You will find rest in the love he sings over you. My prayer is that you will begin to discover God's voice in your life not just as a whisper but also as an echo, and that you'll experience a contagious spiritual awakening that can only come from knowing God.

Blessings,
Margaret

.001 i love you

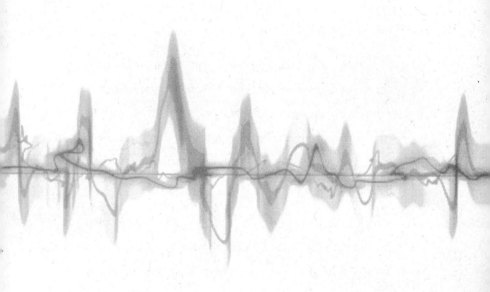

My mother is a natural lifelong learner, a lover of knowledge, and a hardcore trivia buff. Growing up, I was often annoyed by my mother's in-depth knowledge of everything from rock formations to sea life to plant growth. I considered her information addiction annoying at best, except for one small problem: I turned out just like her.

Now I experience the same mini-high when I learn something new or make a discovery. I want to share my connect-the-dot moments with everyone I meet—whether they want to hear them or not. I am my mother's daughter. Because of my info-neurosis, I actually keep a file of news stories in my desk to satisfy my trivia addiction.

Some of the articles in my file simply confirm what most of us already know. Like, did you know teens average an hour more of sleep each night than their parents? I have the study to prove it. Some of the clippings are reminders that small things can make a big difference. For instance, did you know that the average American tosses out seven and a half pounds of garbage each day? Seems like a good reason to recycle. Some of the clippings just make me feel better about myself. One of my all-time favorites, "Fat-bottomed Girls Are Smarter," includes a study of more than 16,000 women that found curvy girls (and their moms) outscored skinny chicks on standardized tests. Now that's good trivia.

One of the articles that recently made its way into my collection was on bat sonar. Random, I know, but that goes with the territory of being an info-maniac. Bats fascinate scientists because of their ability to see in the dark using the echoes of their ultrasonic calls. They send out a frequency that illuminates the environment so they can travel safely in the dark. Pretty cool. While most bats emit their ultrasonic calls from their mouths, about 300 species fire it out of their noses. The process is called echolocation.

Like most snappy words, echolocation percolates in my mind because of its precision in describing a scientifically inexplicable process. Additional research reveals that scientists are still grappling to understand a lot about bats. For example, if a bat is feeding in the dark and you throw a pebble in its trajectory, the creature will dodge the rocky bullet. But if a large insect crosses the same bat's trajectory, the bat will fly toward the savory snack. In less than a second, a bat is able to determine whether he's encountering food or foe. Even with modern technology and gizmos, scientists still can't create a device that emulates what a bat does naturally.

Sandwiched safely in my file drawer, the story piques my

spiritual imagination. When it comes to prayer, all too often, I feel like a bat with broken sonar. I go through life when something unidentifiable—a decision, an opportunity, a possibility—enters my trajectory. I don't know how to respond. At the last possible moment, I finally remember to cry out, *"God, is this a trap or a treat?"*

Thwack!

It's like I'm flying in the dark with regards to my relationship with God. Though I have a hunch he's there somewhere, I can't see him. I do what comes naturally. I let out a sound, a solo prayer, and wait to see what, if anything, comes back.

Like echolocation, there's a lot about the process of prayer that's still a mystery.

I wish prayer was simple, clean, and clear instead of complex, messy, and complicated. I wish hearing from God was as easy as clipping articles and slipping them into a drawer. Then, I could simply open a file anytime and find the exact answer, direction, and encouragement I needed in the moment.

Instead, I find myself calling out to God, hoping he's listening, fingers crossed for a reply. Some people call that faith. For me, it's desperation. The very act of prayer demands vulnerability—an acknowledgement that I don't have all (if any) of the answers, I can't do things on my own, and I'm in need. Intimate prayer is disrobing.

Sometimes after I've poured my head and heart out to God, I'll take a breath long enough to ask, *"God, what's on your heart?"*

On more occasions than I can remember, I have experienced a single word response to this question as an echo in my soul:

You.

Like a feather gently resting on a silky blanket, the word lies soft and tender on my soul. In my heart and mind, it's like God is saying, *I love you.* In those moments, the concerns and weights I've unleashed in prayer disappear, and I am enveloped in the height, depth, and width of God's love. I find myself caught up in praise, worship, and adoration. I don't want to leave; I don't want to let go of thanking God. Though my desire for God is great, it's sadly not long until I lose that sense of wonder in the midst of daily duties. Like a hotline to God, prayer is available throughout the day, but I find myself forgetting to pick up the phone.

In my mind, I know that God loves me every day, but it's far too rare when I feel it in my heart. When those occasions arrive, I want to savor them like the finest chocolate.

As far as my relationship with God, I sometimes feel like Dory in the animated movie *Finding Nemo* or Lucy (played by Drew Barrymore) in *50 First Dates*. Wide-eyed and playful, I have chronic spiritual short-term memory loss. Almost as if each time God speaks, it's just like the first time—even if he's said something a dozen times before. I sit in wonder of God's voice—in the depth, the resolution, and the awe of the encounter. Then, I stop long enough to think, "Hey, that sounds familiar! I think I've heard something like that before."

I love you. Oh yeah! God really does love me!

In his grace, God reminds me once again that his love is true, his love is real. In those moments, I can't help but wonder, *God, why do you have to keep telling me you love me? Shouldn't I already know that by now? Am I just spiritually forgetful or is there something more?*

I've been so bothered by this issue that I have turned to friends, fellow followers, and even Bible scholars to try to decipher why. Most respond with some variation of the same answer: God uses repetition, because you don't hear him the first time.

While that answer contains truth, something about the explanation feels thin to me. The idea that God speaks repetitively because we're slow to comprehend essentially paints a portrait of God's children as toddlers. While there may be some truth in that as evidenced by my own Dory-and-Lucy-like tendencies, I'm not satisfied with the answer. I read of too many men and women in the Bible, including Noah, Abraham, and Mary, who responded to God's voice the first time.

A thicker, more substantial answer is that God speaks

frequently and repetitively because we're so easily distracted. Like a surprise guest at a party, distraction can make a stealth entrance at an opportune time and steal the show. Maybe one of the primary reasons God echoes is so we keep our focus on the most important, not just the most imminent.

While that response makes more sense in my mind and heart, I have a hunch that the reason behind the sacred echo goes even deeper: God is relationally driven. The sacred echo emanates simply out of who he is and his desire to connect with us. Think about it for a moment: Why does God speak the same core messages throughout Scripture? *I love you. I love you. I love you.*

Most, if not all, of the sacred echoes of God throughout the Bible orbit around the idea of relationship. God offers countless incentives for engaging in a relationship with him and strategically instructs us to avoid any attitudes or activities that impede that relationship. Indeed, God is relationally driven. He whispers, he speaks, and he echoes, because he wants to be with us in thought, word, and deed.

That's why when I open the Bible I don't just find instructions for life or a history book, but I also discover a series of love letters. From Genesis to Revelation, God's love expresses itself in countless ways, stories, and lives. God and his love are manifested in the person of Jesus and demonstrated through his life, death, resurrection, and promise of imminent return.

Why use sixty-six books and thousands of years of history
to say three simple words? Because "I love you" is not just a
piece of information or one-time revelation but an invitation to
transformation.

I think about my own relationship with my husband, Leif.
Sometime while we were dating, he spoke the words "I love
you" for the first time. Now this is embarrassing, but I don't
remember exactly when that happened, where we were, or
how I responded. (And yes, I feel like a *total* loser for that one.)
But I do remember him faithfully and graciously pursuing me.
I remember him not just respecting but encouraging a mutual
desire for purity. I remember that fateful day when I collected
twenty-three roses on a rocky trail in Alaska only to discover
two dozen more roses, a diamond ring, and the man who became my husband waiting at the end of the hike. I remember
the desktop file I have with hundreds of love notes Leif
has typed on my computer since we were first married. And
I remember him saying "I love you" this morning. Like any
beloved bride will tell you, all of those expressions of love—
written and spoken and demonstrated—have transformed
me in ways I still cannot fully comprehend.

But what if Leif had taken a different approach? What if he had
whispered the words "I love you" years ago and never spoken
them again? What if he had never written any love notes? Or
expressed that love in kindness, tenderness, and action? What

if I was merely tolerated and not truly loved? How would our relationship be different? How would I be different?

I don't want to know.

God's desire for transformation is one of the foundational reasons for the sacred echo. If God is simply a source for direction or short-term guidance, then is he really much different than the guy behind the information desk in a crowded airport? I may stop by for a recommendation if I'm in pinch, but I'm not going to hang around, let alone invite him on my journey.

God's wisdom and instruction are more than info-to-go. When we view God as just a source of information, then our understanding of him becomes myopic and we forget that God's words are not merely words, but life to be ingested. They nourish our souls. And he is the source of all life. When we focus on mere information, we lose touch with the reality that God's words contain unfathomable power.

In only a few words, God *spoke* creation into existence.

Let there be light. *Let* there be an expanse in the midst of the waters, and *let* it separate the waters from the waters. If you read this account of creation in the first chapter of Genesis, God uses the word "let" more than a dozen times as if he was unleashing something that already existed within him. With mere words, God created. Except for the moment when Jesus spoke, "It is finished," never has so much been accomplished in so few words.

In less than 250 words, God spoke the stars, planets, solar systems, galaxies, heavens, earth, clouds, seas, lakes, puddles, cliffs, dunes, caverns, twigs, petals, giraffes, zebras, polar bears, flamingos, puppies, the human race into existence. If God can do so much with so few words, then I can't afford to miss a single one. As demonstrated in creation and throughout the Bible, the words of God are life, they bring life, they instill life, they bring back to life. His words come alive not just in our minds, but in our hearts, as a holy reverberation of transforming power.

When God echoes *I love you*, it's not a slice of information but a feast of transformation. I am invited to experience the fullness of God's love in my life, heart, and spirit. The holy metamorphosis is designed to ring so genuine and true that others can't help but notice. When *I love you* is alive in my heart, I become freer to love others. When *I love you* is alive in my mind, I become better at expressing that love. When *I love you* is alive in my life, I become a smidgen closer to being who God has called and created me to be.

I can't help but think of Hosea, a prophet whose life was a poignant message of what it looks like to fall in love with God. Hosea was instructed to marry a prostitute named Gomer. The sketchy relationship was a physical manifestation of a spiritual reality: God's people had forgotten their first love.

Even today the book of Hosea remains an invitation to fall head over heels in love with God. I love the words of Hosea:

So let us know, let us press on to know the Lord.
His going forth is as certain as the dawn;
And He will come to us like the rain,
Like the spring rain watering the earth.

Something inside my soul comes alive at the thought of God coming to us like the rain. Spring rain is not just an idea, but a wet experience in awakening, redemption, and restoration that cleanses and brings new life. I ache for God's love to be more than an intellectual assertion in my life. I long to be flooded with his love.

One of the women who I have a hunch experienced the flood of God's love is the poor widow who dropped two thin coins, not even worth a penny, into the temple offering. According to Old Testament laws of inheritance, a widow was prevented from receiving anything from her husband's estate. She was dependent on the gifts of others for her own survival. Though rich people made sizable donations to the temple, Jesus noted that the widow put in more than anyone else. While they gave out of their abundance, she gave out of her poverty—everything she had to live on. Swept up in the moment, she wasn't thinking about what tomorrow would bring or where her next meal would come from.

I used to read this story as a lesson in generosity and giving, but now I recognize this as a love story. The widow gave everything, not with any sense of expectation or entitlement from God, but with deep faith, breathless adoration, and extravagant love. The message of this passage is not to sell everything you own, like that found in Luke, but to give all you have out of love for God. The coins she offered were merely a physical manifestation of her holy affection. She was a living testimony of loving God.

How many times did the widow hear God echo *I love you*? Perhaps the widow's gift was a response that declared *And I love you too!* after years of hearing God echo *I love you*. Like the widow, I need to hear God whisper those words to me regularly, to have them flood my soul lest I become distracted and abandon this foundational truth.

I recently found myself living in overdrive. Waking up early, I breezed through my daily prayer and study, so I could work more. As a result, the quality of my relationship with God diminished. He knew it and I knew it. After all, it's hard to keep secrets from God.

One night I had a dream in which I was sitting before a prominent Bible teacher. We were talking about the daily pressures of balancing family, work, and ministry. We discussed the financial pressures of her television ministry, the challenges of managing her staff, and the stress she faced. I looked at the weightiness of her ministry and asked, "How do you do it?"

She walked toward me, looking me straight in the eye. She held up her index finger and middle finger in the shape of "V" and pointed at my eyes, then her own. Drawing a straight line back and forth between her eyes and my own, she said, "This is the most important thing. If you lose this with Christ, you lose everything."

I woke up. Unlike my usual dreams, I awoke highly alert, the images still vivid in my mind. I moved my right hand using the same gesture I had seen in the dream. The simple motion reminded me of the importance of deep intimacy with God. I lay awake in the humble awe of God's tremendous love, the words, *I love you*, fiery alive in my heart.

Why did God choose to reveal himself to me that night in a dream? And why did the dream feature a prominent teacher? Maybe I had glossed over the passages that had delivered the same message. Maybe I had responded too flippantly to my husband's urgings, "Did you spend time with God this morning?" Maybe I had ignored the passages, the signs, the promptings. Maybe it had been too long since I had experienced God's love. Whatever the cause, God designed a dream to get my attention.

More and more I'm discovering that God doesn't want me

just to know about his love but to experience it. We do not serve a God who is far off, but one who is near and reveals himself and his love in tangible ways. Throughout the Bible we see God using all types of encounters to reveal himself. It's all too easy to read Scripture as a series of stories, bypassing the truth that these were genuine people having authentic encounters with God. When God parted the Red Sea for the Israelites, thousands of people felt squishy mud between their toes. When a group of wise men became mesmerized by a heavenly beauty in the sky, they followed its light and discovered the Son of God. When Jesus said, "Look at the fields! They are ripe for harvest," he and his followers were actually smelling gluten-filled fields of grain. When Peter walked the sea, he felt water as an unfrozen solid for a brief moment. The adventures of Jesus are not merely story; they are experiential.

God invites us to experience him and his love. That is not just an idea or an argument. That's not just the basis for an article to file in the drawer next to my desk. It's a present reality. Though many days I still feel like I am flying in the dark in regards to my relationship with God, I'm grateful that on occasion glimmers of light and echoes of God's persistent voice remind my heart that his love is real.

I love you is just the beginning of an awakening.

.002 sing it again

Focus. You've got to focus, I keep telling myself. The command dissolves into a prayer, *Dear God, help me focus*.

Before I realize what's happening, my eyes drift and I find myself calculating the number of folds in an up-and-down shade in our living room window. I count to twenty-six before losing interest. *Focus, Margaret. You've got to focus.*

When I'm forced to sit still in the silence, distraction becomes all the more appealing. Details that normally escape my notice, like the thickness of dust on the baseboards or shifting of leaves on the oak tree in front of our home, suddenly take on great importance and become wildly entertaining.

Prayer has a way of making my mind dance with ideas and unleashing a creative force inside of me. Like lightning in a still desert, my mind flashes with glimpses of everything I could and should do as well as everything I have left undone. I keep a notebook nearby, jotting down these luminous, loud entries, in an effort to quiet the mind while awakening the spirit. My desire to converse both in the ebb of listening and flow of speaking with God runs deep, and I am dismayed that the mere thought of defrosting chicken breasts for dinner can be so distracting.

My mind still jumpy, I return to the well-worn prayer page in the back of my Bible. My soul tenderly embraces the names I have written there, lifting them up to God, petitioning once again for each person's protection, redemption, and provision. On days like today, the list becomes invaluable—helping me to focus, reminding me of who and what to pray for, no matter the distraction.

The morning confirms what I've known for years—that it's better for me to begin prayer by talking to God rather than listening. If I can get everything off my chest in front of God, then I'm in a better position to listen to whatever is on his mind and heart. More mature men and women who pray may suggest a different route, but I've found this simple pattern works for me. I'm discovering that if you find something that works for you in prayer, then by all means, do it, do it, and keep doing it.

As I look over the names on the page of my Bible, faces of familiar people flash through my mind. I can't help but notice the repetition. The same requests. The same petitions. The same praises I've been offering for years now. Sometimes I secretly wonder, *Does God ever get distracted listening to me? Does God ever get bored with my prayers?*

If God has heard it all before, does he really want to hear it again?

As I've wrestled through this issue, I can't help but think of some of the repetitive prayers of the Bible. When Jesus was asked how to pray, he answered with the words we know as the "Lord's Prayer," one of the most recited prayers in history. In Revelation, we get a glimpse into the heavenly realm where, in a rich blend of prayer, adoration, and worship, four living creatures never cease declaring, "Holy, holy, holy is the Lord God, the Almighty, who was and who is and who is to come." In my own life, the Aaronic blessing has become a daily expression of prayer. Each night, Leif and I tuck ourselves into bed and pray the following over each other:

> *The Lord bless you, and keep you;*
> *The Lord make His face shine on you,*
> *And be gracious to you;*
> *The Lord lift up His countenance on you,*
> *And give you peace.*

Sometimes this simple, rote prayer launches us into a time of holy vespers. Other times, it's just the final words we share before we drift off to sleep.

I can't help but wonder, *does God ever get tired of hearing the same prayers?*

A recent candlelight service helped me answer this question, as my heart discovered what my head already knew. On Christmas Eve, our extended family decided to attend a late evening service. We visited a local sanctuary packed with families of all ages. Young and old had gathered to celebrate the birth of a boy. Though most people who attended could accurately guess the songs we were going to sing and the topic of the message, they came anyway. They weren't looking for that which was different but that which was familiar.

As expected, the sermon focused on the good news that accompanied the birth of Jesus. While the topic was not new, I found myself hanging on the teacher's every word as if she was telling me something I had never heard before. Though well-versed in the story, I found the teaching encouraging, inspiring, and engaging. Not only did I need to hear the good news again, but I was also reminded of the importance of letting others know too.

One of the stories the preacher shared still sticks with me. A young boy and his father were shopping at the mall. After only a few stores, the boy had grown tired and fussy. In an effort to keep the boy's crankiness at bay, the father picked up his son, pressed him tightly against his chest in a bear-like hug, and began singing a random, original song over his child. The lyrics blended phrases like, "I love you," "You are my son," "I love being with you," and "You and me together." Though the lyrics lacked rhyme and the song lacked rhythm, the young boy sat calmly in his father's arms for the remainder of the shopping expedition.

As they were leaving the mall and making their way to the car, the young boy looked up into his father's eyes and said, "Sing it again, Daddy. Sing it again!" The words sung by his father were not tiresome; rather, they reminded the boy of his father's love.

At the close of the service, each person's candle was individually lit. The lights lowered, and a thousand strangers and I sang "Silent Night" in luminous beauty and humble awe. As the final chorus came to a close, I found myself wishing, *Can we sing it again? Please, let's sing it again.*

Leaving the service, I was filled with all the bountiful joy that accompanies the wonder of the holiday season. An unexpected Christmas gift, the words *Sing it again!* have not left me. They have become a sacred echo, a reminder of God's desire for me and my desire for God.

The words of my heavenly father are not tiresome, but instead remind me of God's faithfulness. Like the young boy, I love to hear my heavenly father's voice. Those moments when I hear him echo through Scripture make me come alive. God's every word breathes life into my soul. No matter what God uses—whether a Bible passage, a sermon, or a Christmas Eve service—I am grateful for the moments when God draws my heart back to his. Like the young boy, my spirit cries out, *Sing it again, Abba. Sing it again!*

One of the passages of Scripture that I never get tired of hearing, reading, or studying is found in Isaiah. Though the passage describes the redemption of Israel, I feel my own redemption being described. As my eyes pass over the words, phrases arrest my attention and apprehend my heart:

> *Thus says the Lord ... He who formed you ... Do not fear ... I have redeemed you ... I have called you by name ... You are Mine ... I will be with you ... I am the Lord your God ... Your Savior ... You are precious in My sight ... You are honored ... I love you ... Do not fear ...*

Though I read that passage a thousand times, my heart cries out, *Sing it again.* Those words of Scripture never grow old. Like God's promises, they are new every morning. Yet despite their freshness and life, distraction sometimes still gets the best of me.

Sometimes I think that our greatest challenge as followers of God is not having too little information but too much. The Bible makes it clear that God wants us to be able to recognize his voice.

Scripture overflows with examples of God speaking to his people. Adam, Eve, Abraham, Moses, David, Samuel, and Noah all experienced ongoing dialogue with God. Yet God doesn't just speak to the big-name, biblical equivalent of rock stars; he spoke to Cain regarding his countenance, Hagar regarding her son, and Ananias regarding a blind persecutor of the church. Meanwhile, Jesus personalized the idea of conversation with God. He demonstrated through his life that hearing God's voice was more of an expectation than an exception.

I believe that we will never be better able to discern God's voice from the other voices as quickly, concisely, or accurately as when we spend time in God's Word. This is where God most often "sings it again." Published as the greatest love letter of all time, the Bible is a soul-wrenching invitation to a real relationship with the one who can love us like no other. Whether we read the words in an ancient or modern transla-tion or download an audio version on our iPod, God's Word breathes life and provides jettys of hope. Specific passages provide the correction and direction we need. When we allow the words of God to come alive in our hearts, they unleash an unmistakable transforming power in our attitudes and actions.

One of my all-time favorite definitions of prayer comes from Clement of Alexandria who simply described the divine activ-ity as "keeping company with God." Not only are we servants of God, but by his grace he has also made us friends, so that we serve him out of gratitude. Through prayer, we partner with God in the work he is doing throughout the earth.

Through prayer, God invites us to sing the song of our lives to him—every word and every phrase—and he even enjoys the chorus. Prayer matters. Sometimes that's easy to forget, especially when I don't see any answers, or worse, when I receive an answer I didn't really want. Yet the invitation remains:

Sing it again.

I am beginning to believe the real beauty of prayer is not just in the request but in the repetition. Something wondrous happens when we respond to the admonition of Paul to pray without ceasing. Something enchanting happens when we ask God for something more than once, as if with each refrain, our heart aligns itself a shade closer to God's heart. It's almost as if something sacred happens in the echo of our prayers. Through prayer we become part of a greater story—the story of what God is doing in our lives, our families, our communities, and around the world.

Why pray when God has heard it all before? Because God really does answer prayer. The same God who is sovereign and immutable and knows everything from the beginning to the end, not only gives us his ear, but he invites us to take it as well. Though the answers he gives are not always the ones we hope for, God still invites us to pray. And he delights in every syllable. Our highly relational God wants to keep company with us and that involves responding to us even when the answers and timing are not exactly what we want to hear.

Why pray? Because something inherently changes inside of us when we persist in prayer. When I was living in Florida, I met a guy named Finn who managed to get on my last nerve. He floated among our group of friends, and often left me flabbergasted by his confrontational nature. During our initial encounter, he criticized my lack of conservative attire (since I was wearing shorts instead of pants) and attacked various points of my belief system since they didn't reflect his über-conservative perspective. I discovered our first meeting was just his warm-up act. Over the next few months, he appeared at my door uninvited around dinner time to find out what I was going to cook for him, asked for rides around town at inconvenient times, and borrowed items on multiple occasions without returning them.

I experienced the full spectrum of anger and frustration toward my nemesis. I wanted to say "el fin" to Finn forever, except for one little problem: he was a Christian. And I couldn't shake the sense that God had brought him into my life to change something in me. After six months of knowing Finn, my nerves were shredded. As many times as I took him and the situation to God in prayer, I couldn't shake the anger. One day during my time of prayer and study, I stumbled on an often quoted verse from the Sermon on the Mount: "But I say to you who hear, love your enemies, do good to those who hate you."

How could I possibly love Finn? I knew Finn didn't hate me, but I was well on my way to hating him. How could my heart change? As I read these words, I cried out to God. A thought entered my mind that was clearly not my own: *Help Finn pay for his tuition to Bible college.*

Are you kidding, God? I had a laundry list of reasons why the suggestion was ridiculous, including Finn's need to take personal responsibility and grow up. Yet I knew the issue wasn't really about Finn, it was about my heart. The next day, I went down to the local Bible college and made an anonymous donation to help cover Finn's tuition for the semester.

I'd love to tell you that was a turning point in Finn's life, but honestly nothing changed. He still showed up late to events, made inappropriate comments, and continued in what can only be described as leech-like behavior. Yet something changed inside of me. His rude comments lost their sting. His inappropriate behavior became forgivable and even endearing in rare moments. I began to see beyond Finn's prickly exterior and discover a guy who had lost both of his parents, grew up in foster care, survived multiple abusive situations, and was quietly grateful for every opportunity, every friend, every warm meal. Over the following months, I found myself growing a new heart for Finn, and we became friends. This was a direct result of persistent prayer and God's grace-filled answer.

Through prayer I discover things about myself and God I could not discover any other way. Prayer provides a mirror to my soul. Through prayer, my motives and attitudes are brought to the light. Through prayer, I can explore the source of my less-than-becoming behavior. Along the way I discover unsuspected roots of unforgiveness, agreement with things that simply aren't true, and places of woundedness that otherwise go unnoticed, and worse, unhealed.

Through prayer, I discover the shadows of my sin and recognize the luminescence of God's redemption and restoration. During prayer, my eyes shift from self-focus to God-awareness, and I find myself with a heavenly perspective that is not my own. Looking at life through God's perspective changes everything. When my eyes are locked on him, I discover a God who is not only bighearted but also outrageously generous, abundantly kind, and surprisingly talkative. Through this lens, my behemoth issues and rickshaw weaknesses gain proper perspective.

Through prayer, I answer the call of Hebrews 12:2 to fix my eyes on Jesus, the author and perfecter of my faith, and I am empowered not only to see more clearly but also to obey more readily.

Not only do I need to hear God's voice, but also he wants to hear mine. In those mornings when I pour my soul out to him in prayer, I find the words echoing in my heart and mind,

Sing it again, Margaret.

Sing it again—because I hear you, and I love you more than you could know.

On those walks when I praise God for the beauty of his creation at the sight of a deer or elk or wild bunny, does not God cry out,

Sing it again, Margaret, Sing it again?

On those evenings when my husband and I tuck ourselves into bed with the love, beauty, unity intended for marriage and pray the ancient prayer that God has heard thousands of times before, does he not whisper, *Sing it again, Margaret, Sing it again?*

No wonder the phrase, *Sing it again*, keeps coming alive in my heart and mind. The sacred echo is a gentle reminder to pray and keep praying, to listen and keep listening—no matter what the distractions.

My mind begins to wander. *Focus, Margaret. You've got to focus.*

After all, there is more to be prayed for this day.

.003 how long?

If prayer is one part speaking and one part listening, I think there's a third part people don't talk about as often: waiting. As my eyes glance over the list of prayer requests, I realize that I've been sitting in the waiting room of prayer for many years.

On this particular morning, Meredith, a friend I've known for more than a decade, stood out on my list. Smart, sweet, and beautiful, she is one of those women you can't spend more than five minutes without thinking she is going to be an amazing mother one day. As a nurse at a children's hospital, her ability to love, nurture, and encourage kids is constantly on display. She embodies many of the characteristics of the woman described in Proverbs 31: resourceful, generous, full of dignity and integrity.

Over the years, I've watched her handle singleness with poise and grace. Though her heart's desire has always been marriage and family, she has refused to put her life on hold. Instead, she spends her time, money, and energy serving and loving others.

As I bring her before the Father this day, I'm echoing a request he has heard a thousand times before, *Will you please bring her a husband?*

The prayer carries extra weight as I hand it over to God, because I have tasted the bittersweetness that comes with waiting for a spouse. Though I was never one of those gals who went to bed with wedding bells dancing in her head, I remember waking up sometime around the age of twenty-seven and thinking, *I want to be married.*

Marriage seemed like the natural next step in life, and my prayers for a spouse joined the prayers of family and friends who had been petitioning God on my behalf for years. When the answer didn't come quickly, I transitioned from actively living to passively waiting. My verve for life waned, subtly stripping life of its Technicolor. These muted moments were most noticeable when life was at its best. Adventurous road trips, breathtaking sunrises, and lazy afternoons underneath a snuggly down comforter just reminded me of a hollowness I felt in my soul. The prayer for a spouse became a dull ache with the occasional shooting pain. Some prayers you don't need to write down to remember, and others you don't write down lest you remember. This was one of those scandalous prayers: *God, I did what you asked in pursuing a relationship with you. I've kept myself pure—serving, loving, traveling, working—living life trying to follow you, obey you, honor you.*

But where is he? Why isn't he here? Why aren't you keeping up your part of the bargain?

Though my own prayers were answered, I can still feel a phantom pain when I speak my friend's name, an aching reminder of what it's like to wait on God. That's when the heart question emerges, *Why is my beautiful, fabulous, and lovely friend still single despite an unquenchable desire to be a wife and mother, years of patiently waiting on God, and thousands upon thousands of prayers by friends and family? And why do I find myself praying the same prayers for so many others?*

As I look down the prayer list, I see lives where God has faithfully and abundantly answered with a spouse, but so many others are still waiting and hoping. I have a hunch that they sometimes feel the same dull ache. I can't help but echo the same prayer: *Why, God? Why?*

Though I pray repetitively, vehemently, I hear the thick silence, like that which follows the dropping of a heavy, leather-bound book onto a hard, wooden library floor. I am gently reminded that these people I know, these precious names, are not the only ones waiting. Whether single, married, young, or old, we're all waiting.

Maybe, in some ways, we're supposed to feel the ache, a welcome reminder that this is not our home. I find myself circling an even deeper question:

Why so much waiting?

Thumbing through Scripture, I can't help but notice that
waiting is woven into the fabric of history. God is waiting.
Creation is waiting. Humankind is waiting. We are all waiting
for redemption, for everything to be put back in its proper
place in relation to God. We see signs and shadows, aches
and groans of what's to come, knowing that what we wait
for is not here yet.

Throughout the Bible, a question reverberates:

"How long?"

Those two little words appear more than fifty times, and it's
no wonder, because waiting is part of our story—all of our
stories. Adam and Eve waited, fresh fruit staining their faces,
for God to discover what they had done. Noah waited for the
first few delicate raindrops to pitter-patter on his odd-shaped
boat. Abram waited for a promised son, Jacob waited for a
promised wife, and the Israelites waited for a promised new
life.

Yet the first person to ask this question outright was neither
prophet nor pilgrim but God himself. In Exodus 10:3, Moses
and Aaron deliver God's question to Pharaoh: "This is what
the Lord, the God of the Hebrews, says: "How long will you
refuse to humble yourself before Me? Let My people go, that
they may serve Me."

I find great comfort knowing that God is concerned about the length of our captivity—both in Egypt and in a fallen world embedded with sin—and that he feels the ache too. God knew the answer to his own question but asked it anyway.

If the Father of time asks "How long?" how much more will we?

Two types of waiting await us in life. The first is The Great Wait —that moment when the trumpet will sound and the Jesus who rode into Jerusalem on a donkey will return on a white horse. Like townspeople in an ancient city, we wait for the return of our King who will bring with him redemption, restoration, and reward. We will celebrate wildly at the wedding of the ages—that great feast in the banquet hall of heaven that God has been preparing since the beginning of time.

When I look into the eyes of my friend's mom who is battling cancer, I feel the ache of The Great Wait. When I listen to the stories of pastors who carry their people's burdens as their own, I feel the ache of The Great Wait. And when I listen to the stories of chronic pain and abuse in the lives of so many, I feel the ache of The Great Wait. At those moments, my prayers join the chorus, "How long?"

Though I've asked the same questions many times, only recently have I found God turning the question around on me. Like a sacred echo, I find God asking me,

How long?

That may seem like a strange question for the One who fixes epochs to ask, but I find those two words pulling against my soul and inviting me into a deeper relationship with God; they remind me that I am not alone. I am not just waiting for God but with God. My heart longs for redemption, restoration, and reconciliation. I want sickness to be eliminated, peace throughout the earth, and the world to be put in proper order. As much as I desire these things, God desires them even more. When these two words come alive in my heart, I know God is still with me and still to be trusted.

I'm humbled to admit that most days I'm less concerned with The Great Wait and more concerned with the second kind of waiting, My Personal Wait, which usually ends up focusing on whatever is next. You probably have a My Personal Wait list of your own. Sometimes the list includes a life stage—like marriage, buying a home, or having children—but often it's a more common event, much like the changing of the seasons or tides.

As I run my finger down my prayer list, I recognize so many others living in the same undertow, waiting on spouses, jobs, homes, transfers, graduations, healings, and reconcili-ations. Waiting always leads to the same place: *In-between*. Sometimes I think the place of *In-between* is one of the most gnarly, dark places in life because you aren't fully here and you aren't fully there. Emotions, hopes, and dreams are strewn across a seemingly endless list of possibilities and potentials. When you're *In-between*, the next jetty of hope could be moments away. Or not. Emotions run forward, and fears hold back. Seams of uncertainty can burst at any given second. If you stay in the undercurrent very long, sometimes you can feel like you're losing yourself.

My Personal Wait list is miles long. As soon as I cross one thing off the list, two more appear. I remember the cycle of waiting as a child for the next birthday or holiday. Whether we were living in Florida, North Carolina, or Colorado, I remember waiting for the finish of a school year or the beginning of the next. I remember waiting eagerly the spring of my senior year for acceptance into a small liberal arts school in North Carolina. Ironically, I ended up on the wait list. Once accepted, I made the transition into college life only to wait for the transition into the real world. Since I was a child, My Personal Wait list has just been growing longer and leads me to the place of *In-between*.

Topping My Personal Wait list most recently was a new job for my husband and best friend, Leif. Though Alaska was his home state and a place we both called home for almost five years, we both felt the pull to return to the lower forty-eight. For more than two years, he applied for work in a variety of states, lacing each application with prayer. Still no job. Mailing out résumés was easy enough, but the possibility of moving raised all kinds of questions regarding our relationships and involvement in the local community. How much do we take on? How much do we get involved? How much do we invest in people when we know we might be leaving? How long are we going to be here?

For more than two years, we were caught in this riptide of *In-between*—waiting for what's next but not knowing when and if it will come. Eventually, we packed up and left Alaska without a job for my husband. Everything worked out, but not in the way we anticipated.

At times, the reality of *In-between* is downright scary— that place of blind trust where the precepts of faith meet the narrow path of fortitude, and movement is demanded though there's no definitive place to go but forward. The worst part about *In-between* isn't the uncertainty, discouragement, or frustration, but that sometimes I think God likes it when we're there.

While he shares no traits with a sadist, sometimes I think God loves the tension of *In-between*. He loves what it does to us—the humility it creates within our hearts. The prayers that emerge from our spirits. The childlike cries from our innermost beings that acknowledge utmost dependence. Maybe that's why he allows us to enter *In-between* and cry out *How long?* In that place, we face the unflinching question:

What will we do with the time?

That's a hard question to answer—whether we're facing The Great Wait or My Personal Wait. I feel like telling God, *In case you haven't noticed by now, I'm a "C" student when it comes to this, so can we just move onto the next subject?*

He looks down from heaven, smiles, and schedules another delay.

Will I dig in, making the most of what I have been given for however long I have been given it, or will I pull back, afraid to make promises that I simply can't keep? That's the wrestling match I have with my soul every day—to be fully present, vested in the here and now, no matter what may come. Some days I fare better than others.

Over the last few years, I've noticed that the process of waiting that accompanies prayer brings impurities like fear, lack of faith, and doubt to the surface of my soul. Once exposed, I hand them back to God in a blend of confession, repentance, and celebration, grateful for the knowledge that God's still at work inside me.

When I think of waiting, I can't help but think of John the Baptist, the fulfillment of a 400-year-old prophecy, standing on the muddy shores of the Jordan River wearing the wardrobe of Elijah and welcoming the Messiah. Not only did John immerse Jesus and watch the heavens open and the Spirit of God descend in the form of a dove, but he also heard the audible voice of God speak, "This is My beloved Son, in whom I am well-pleased."

Those are the kinds of days you never forget unless, of course, you find yourself in the murky waters of *In-between*. For John, that place was a prison cell, a physical holding tank where the darkness of confinement, deplorable conditions, and daily waiting brought doubts and fears to the surface. If the place of *In-between* can make the forerunner of Christ wonder if he had missed his mark, what can it do to you or me?

Rumors of his cousin's work made their way into John's cell, and he sent his own followers to ask Jesus, "Are You the Expected One, or shall we look for someone else?"

For John, this was not just a head question, but a heart question. He had banked his life, ministry, *everything*, on delivering the news that the much awaited One had arrived. Yet even after experiencing the ultimate baptism, doubt—the kind that makes you question everything you believe—still surfaced in John's heart.

Familiar with the political and religious climate of the day, John's question is a sort of code. Only those familiar with the teachings of Jesus could decipher "the one who was to come."

Interestingly, Jesus answers the question the same way: "Go

and report to John what you hear and see: the blind receive sight and the lame walk, the lepers are cleansed and the deaf hear, and the dead are raised up, and the poor have the gospel preached to them."

Rather than give a clear answer, Jesus' response refers to prophecies found in the book of Isaiah, six specific signs the Messiah will fulfill when he comes. Jesus knew that John knew them by heart: The blind receive sight, the lame walk, those who have leprosy are cleansed, the deaf hear, the dead are raised, and the good news is preached to the poor.

What captures my attention in Jesus' response is not the six prophecies he fulfilled, but the seventh prophecy he seemingly goes out of his way not to mention: to proclaim freedom for the captives. Answering John's cryptic question in code, Jesus is gently saying that although he is indeed the Messiah, the one who is waited for, John will not be set free.

Jesus' answer leaves me conflicted. I'm comforted to know that Jesus can read between the lines. When we place our deepest doubts and longings before him, he does not shrink back from our concerns—he answers us right where we are, in language we'll understand. But like John the Baptist, I must also face the reality that which I wait for may not always come in this lifetime.

Why so much waiting?

I do not know, but I do know that when God asks,

How long?

he invites us to place the weight of the wait on him. He does not want us to wait alone, but rather to wait on him alone. God invites the restless soul, like my own, to find respite in him. Not only does he listen to our heart's cries as we wait, but he blesses us, strengthens us, and renews us in the process. The reward for the wait is described as immeasurable:

> *For from of old they have not heard or perceived by ear,*
> *Neither has the eye seen a God besides Thee,*
> *Who acts in behalf of the one who waits for Him.*

If waiting packs so many benefits and blessings, then why is it still so hard? Why do I waste time worrying, complaining, and filling every crevice of time with activity? I think I have a lot to learn from Meredith.

As I lift her name to God this day, I find myself thankful for her strength, her resolve, her example of what it means to live well while waiting on him. And I realize that her story is not so much about what God has left undone as it is about what he has done in and through her—the beacon of faith that she has become.

.004 read it again

My mother is a natural lifelong learner, a lover of knowledge, and a hardcore trivia buff. Growing up, I was often annoyed by my mother's in-depth knowledge of everything from rock formations to sea life to plant growth. I considered her information addiction annoying at best, except for one small problem: I turned out just like her.

Before you keep reading, please hit the pause button. Does what you just read sound familiar? You've read it before. These words were the launching pad to the first chapter of this book. Now I need to ask you: Did you recognize these words or gloss by them? Did you think it was a printing mistake? Were you bothered by the repetition? Or did you catch it instantly?

Now the deeper question: Are there any parallels between how you responded to this repetition and how you respond to the repetition of God in your life?

Think about this for moment: How do you respond to the sacred echo in your life? Are you moving too quickly to recognize the ways God is speaking to you? Are you glossing by those moments when God is trying to get your attention? Are you annoyed by the persistence? Or has God's persistence become a welcome friend?

I'm increasingly discovering that whenever God speaks to us it's pause-worthy. It's not just worth taking note, but worth pausing to stop, think, reflect, meditate, and ask questions. God speaking is a hint that something deeper is going on. So when God speaks something to my heart, often through Scripture, I will take time to prayerfully ask him, *What does this mean? Where are you going with this?* I'll ask the Holy Spirit to connect the dots in my life.

The problem is that many days I don't hear anything. I cry out to God only to find myself sitting in deafening silence. I don't feel or sense or experience anything. In an effort to connect with God, I'll open the Scriptures hoping that his word will come alive in my heart. Some days it does, but many days it does not. Instead, it feels flat, mundane, familiar yet distant. The truth of Scripture seems a million miles away with no real relevancy to my life, and I hate that.

More than anything, I hunger to live a God-infused life. Apart from Scripture, it's impossible to live that life to the fullest. So I cry out to God, *Open my eyes to see and ears to hear. What do you want to say to me?*

That's one of those prayers God loves to answer.

Several years ago after praying this prayer I was reading in the book of 2 Samuel the story of Absalom, a man who betrayed his own father, the king. Rather than wait in line for the throne, he took matters into his own hands and organized a coup, forcing King David to flee for his life. In the uprising that followed, Absalom was killed and someone had to deliver the news to David.

One young man, Ahimaaz, eagerly volunteered but was not selected. He was not the one to carry the message that day. A second runner was chosen and began his journey. Ahimaaz pleaded with the leader to let him run. Even though there was no reward, Ahimaaz wanted to deliver the news. When he received permission, he ran fast and hard—cutting across a plain. The shortcut paid off. Ahimaaz reached David first. Eager to know the status of his son, David asked, "Is it well with the young man Absalom?"

"When Joab sent the kings' servant, and your servant, I saw a great tumult, but I did not know what it was," Ahimaaz said, back-pedaling from the truth. Ahimaaz was more concerned with running and giving a message than with actually delivering it.

Unsatisfied with the ambiguous answer, David instructed Ahimaaz to step aside. When the second runner arrived, David repeated the same question: "Is it well with the young man Absalom?"

The second runner faithfully delivered the news: The king's son was dead. David went to his chamber and wept.

After I read the story, I felt an urgency in my mind and spirit,

Read it again.

I studied the story a second time still confused by its importance or meaning.

Read it again, I sensed.

The passage appeared straightforward.

Read it again.

After three readings, the story still lay flat in my mind.

The next day, I was hopeful the passage would come alive.

Read it again.

I faithfully read it again and again but still didn't understand. On the third day I persisted in prayer and study. *Show me, Lord. Open my eyes to see and ears to hear,* I prayed.

The passage came alive for the first time. As I reread the story, I identified with one of the characters. There are times and situations when we all see ourselves as people in the Bible — the prodigal son or his older brother, the impetuous disciple Peter, or the rambunctious Paul. In this particular passage, I found myself identifying with the second runner. While God clearly uses those with great speed, skill, and passion, like Ahimaaz, to build his kingdom and accomplish his will, he also uses those of us who may not be as swift but are still faithful and obedient. On that day, I felt like God was reminding me not to be distracted by the other runners.

Over the years, I cannot count the number of times the passage of the two runners has come alive in my heart. Depending on the circumstance or season, particular aspects of the story will come to mind. Gentle reminders that I am to be true to the King. Gentle echoes that my calling as God's child is secure. Gentle promptings not to get distracted by those around me who may be running faster.

This passage has become a pearl in my life, and I am grateful for the persistent nudge,

Read it again.

All too often I have a tendency to breeze through Scripture without taking the time to dig deeper, reread, and reflect. Yet slowly I'm learning the importance of responding to the echo to read it again. Often in those moments I'll stumble across a scriptural truth I've heard for eons, but only as God illuminates the passage does the message become loud enough for me to finally comprehend not just with my mind but my heart.

I wish this happened every day. I would love it if each time I read the Bible I walked away with a treasure of spiritual awakening and discovery. I wish that simply rereading a passage was the secret to unlocking new vaults of biblical truth every day. While some days rereading unleashes a cache of discovery, all too often weeks and months go by before I find something new. Yet the reward is worth the search and wait.

As I've reflected on the jewels I've gained from Scripture when I've responded to the echo of rereading a passage, I can't help but notice the ways God approaches each of us and how the things he says are deeply personal. Like a father who recognizes the colorful rainbow of personality differences in his own children but still has a special way of connecting with them one-on-one, God does not take a one-size-fits-all approach. Instead, he is intensely personal.

This was readily apparent when Jesus began his public ministry. According to the account of John, Jesus' first converts came through a variety of interactions, experiences, and conversations. The first two disciples discovered Jesus by listening to John the Baptist. They simply began following him. Noticing the innocent stalkers, Jesus turns and asks, "What do you seek?" The would-be disciples answer honestly, if not straightforwardly, "Rabbi, where are you staying?"

Jesus says, "Come, and you will see."

One of the two original disciples, Andrew, couldn't keep his discovery to himself. He quickly finds his brother, Simon and exclaims, "We have found the Messiah."

Jesus never hesitates when it comes to getting personal with his followers. When Jesus sees Simon for the first time, he says, "You are Simon the son of John; you shall be called Cephas (which is translated Peter)."

The very next day, Jesus finds Philip, and with two of my favorite words, "Follow me," the young man leaves everything to become a disciple. Philip can't keep the secret to himself. He finds Nathanael and tells him that they have found the Messiah, Jesus of Nazareth.

Nathanael, skeptical at best, asks, "Can any good thing come out of Nazareth?"

"Come and see," Philip urges.

When Jesus sees Nathanael, he can barely contain his smile, "Behold, an Israelite indeed, in whom is no guile."

"How do you know me?" Nathanael asks.

"Before Philip called you, when you were under the fig tree, I saw you," Jesus responds.

Nathanael is wide-eyed. "Rabbi, You are the Son of God; you are the King of Israel."

"Because I said to you that I saw you under the fig tree, do you believe? You shall see greater things than these. Truly, truly, I say to you, you will see the heavens opened and the angels of God ascending and descending on the Son of Man."

Throughout this passage in John 1, we see people continually giving up their lives to follow Jesus. Yet there's no real formula, no cookie cutter to be found. Each disciple discovers and interacts with Jesus differently. Two of the disciples were given a place to stay. One of the disciples was given a new name, another a straightforward invitation to become a follower. Some of the disciples found Jesus on their faith journey; others discovered Jesus by listening to someone else's faith journey. In every instance, Jesus was incredibly personal.

This is particularly true in the conversion of Nathanael, one of the more ornery and outspoken of the original followers. "Can any good thing come out of Nazareth?" is a zinger of a response any cynic can appreciate. Yet Jesus is not caught off-guard by the snappy comment. He lovingly exposes Nathanael as a guileless man, one without deception or duplicity.

In one of the most cryptic passages of Scripture, Jesus alludes to something that happened to Nathanael under a fig tree. The mere mention results in Nathanael's immediate conversion. What happened under that tree? To this day, no one knows.

I'm glad.

More than anything, the interaction reveals just how intimate and personal God is with us. He says things to us that might be meaningless to someone else, but for us they make all the difference. They make God real and remind us that God is near. When a spiritual truth comes alive in my heart, it transforms me.

As I talk about the sacred echo with friends and ask about their gems of truth, I'm encouraged by how many recognize God's presence in their life. As they dig into Scripture, they unearth deep truths like buried treasures. Among those on my prayer list, I see many who are not only growing in their knowledge of God but in their relationship with him too. Though their specific expressions of faith are different, their expressions of love often look and feel the same.

While studying the Bible, I find myself returning to particular books, stories, and passages. One sermon that I never get tired of reading is the Sermon on the Mount. Sometimes I think I could read this portion of Scripture a bazillion times and still discover something new. Recently, I found three potent questions Jesus asks pause-worthy:

> "Or what man is there among you, when his son shall ask him for a loaf, will give him a stone? Or if he shall ask for a fish, he will not give him a snake, will he? If you then, being

*evil, know how to give good gifts to your children, how
much more shall your Father who is in heaven give what is
good to those who ask Him!"*

Though I had studied this passage many times before, I
felt the gentle nudge to read it again. As I reread, the word
you caught my attention. Suddenly, this wasn't a question
that Jesus was asking the crowds on a dusty mountainside
thousands of years ago, but a question he was asking me.

The questions exposed something inside me: my underlying
fear that maybe God isn't really good. Through this passage,
I began to recognize that mistrust of God was affecting my
prayer life.

My mind began wandering around the phrase "if his son asks
for bread." As God's child, what type of bread am I asking for?
Mere crumbs? Stale crusts? A cheap, generic, low-fat slice that
tastes like sawdust? Or a fresh loaf of crunchy artisan bread
baked with roasted garlic cloves and kalamata olives?

If his son asks for bread, what am I asking God for? In all honesty, a lot of crumby prayers. I'd like to think it's because I'm
maturing in my prayer life. I'm offering God more reasonable
requests. I'm loving my friends, family, and foes more by asking God for those things he naturally wanted to give. Right?

Or am I just praying it safe?

As I reread the passage, I was reminded of the truth: God is more good than I can possibly imagine or comprehend. I guess God never said he would give me *everything* I asked for. Not all my prayers move God to act. Not all my prayers cause God to respond. Not all my prayers seem to have answers.

But what if the next prayer does?

What if the next prayer makes the difference? What if the next prayer is the one that God answers? What if the next prayer is the one that helps change someone's heart or life?

Suddenly, I found my desire to pray and trust God renewed. Pausing over this one passage and reading it again served as a powerful reminder to persist in prayer even when I don't understand, even when I don't comprehend, even in the darkness. Through this one passage, I was filled with a renewed sense that nothing is too big for the One who loves us. I want to tell you that the work in my life is done in this area, but I think it's only the beginning of the awakening.

I recently stumbled on the story of a first-century rabbi known as Honi the Circle-Maker. Now here's a little background from my heritage: Despite the centrality of relationship with God within Judaism, it's not acceptable to appear overly familiar with God. In fact, anyone who acted as if they were too familiar with God could be excommunicated. Yet according to the Mishnah (part of the Talmud), Honi was an exception:

Once they asked Honi the Circle-Maker to pray for rain. He said to them, "Go out and bring in the [clay] ovens so they won't be softened (by the rain)."

He prayed, but no rain fell.

So what did he do? He drew a circle, stood inside it, and said to God, "Master of the Universe, your children have turned to me because they consider me a son in your household. I swear by your great name that I will not move from here until you show compassion on your children!"

A few drops fell.

> "I didn't pray for that kind of rain, but for rain that will fill the ditches, caves and water cisterns."

Rain began falling violently.

> "I didn't pray for that kind of rain either, but for good, pleasant rain that will be a blessing."

Then it began to rain normally and it kept raining so long they had to ask Honi to pray that it stop pouring.

Shim'on ben-Sh'tach (a rabbinic leader) sent a message to him: "If you were anyone except Honi, I would have pronounced a ban of excommunication on you! But what am I to do to you? You beg God and he does what you want, like a son who cajoles his father and he does what he wants."

I love that story, not just because it's a majestic portrait of Jewish culture, tradition, and holy chutzpah, but because it shows that some people have these out-of-the-box or inside-the-circle experiences that remind us that nothing is impossible for God.

Honi's adventure gently reminds me of another rainmaker from the Bible. The epistle of James describes Elijah as a person with a nature like ours who prayed earnestly that it wouldn't rain. His prayers were answered. The land experienced a drought for the next three and a half years. Then Elijah prayed that it would rain. And it poured. Indeed, the effective prayers of the righteous accomplish much.

Throughout Scripture God is constantly revealing facets of himself, luminous discoveries of his love, goodness, and faithfulness. Like crown jewels, they are to be treasured. No matter how clear the initial spiritual impulse may be, I'm learning the importance of pressing God for more. I want all he has to give. I want his full work completed in me. I know that I see things dimly. I need the illumination.

So whenever I hear the echo,

Read it again,

I want to respond, knowing that it's pause-worthy, and discover what our incredibly personal God wants to reveal.

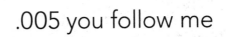

.005 you follow me

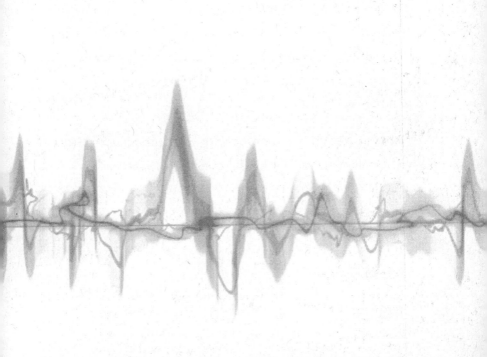

After graduating from college in North Carolina, I spent several years living in Colorado before enrolling in classes at a Bible college in Florida. While I found the lessons inspiring and spiritually challenging, some of the conversations with other students made me tilt my head sideways in bewilderment.

It wasn't uncommon for someone to walk up and ask, "What is God's calling on your life?" The question always made me feel like a tourist without a map.

After stammering for a few moments without any real reply, I'd turn the question around on the interrogator, "What's God's calling on your life?"

Without hesitation, the person would tell me they were destined to be a lead pastor, worship leader, or launch a ministry. I was intrigued and impressed. But the responses that left me the most puzzled were from young women who claimed that God had called them to be a pastor's wife.

"Wow, that's awesome!" I'd reply. "Who's the lucky guy?"

"I'm not dating anyone, but I know God will bring *the one*."

"That's great," I'd affirm, secretly wondering what the young woman was going to do if God tarried.

To this day, I still don't know whether the cause was the demographics of the student population or the culture of the campus, but it seemed like God had spoken to almost everyone I met on one or both of two main issues: who they were going to marry and the worldwide ministry they were called to launch. I don't remember anyone who ever felt like God called them to singleness or to simply serve in the local church without an impressive job title.

God had never spoken to me specifically about marriage or ministry, so I felt out of the loop. Maybe I wasn't praying hard enough. Maybe I wasn't listening long enough. Maybe God was calling me to something completely different, and my dream job of working as a quality control taster at Godiva was still in his plan.

Living in a God-speaks-greatness-into-everyone environment can lead to shadows of self-doubt when God isn't speaking to you. I began to wonder, *God, have you forgotten me? Do you still have a plan for me? Am I doing something I shouldn't be doing or not doing something that I should?* I felt confused and misplaced.

That's when I was introduced to one of those foundational

passages that keeps me from playing hooky in my relationship with God. It's been like a spiritual anchor for me—an ancient crusty truth that sinks hard and fast into my soul. As I prayed about my internal turmoil one morning, I was introduced to John 21, a section of Scripture I had read many times before but never the same way. The passage describes a memorable breakfast on the beach with the already resurrected Jesus and his followers. Simon Peter and his friends are fishing when a familiar voice yells out to them to place their nets on the other side of the boat. Against their better judgment, they follow the advice of the landlocked man and find their nets snapping under the weighty catch. In the midst of the frenzy, Simon Peter is informed that the stranger is Jesus. Throwing on a shirt, he belly flops into the water and swims to shore as fast as he can.

When the water finally grows shallow enough for his feet to touch, Simon Peter spots Jesus standing near a beachside fire. The unmistakable smell of smoke, charred fish, and fresh, baked bread fill the air. This is not an ordinary breakfast, but an encounter that changes one disciple forever and echoes truths into my heart thousands of years later.

This was Simon Peter's day. The young disciple had already experienced the highs and lows of three years of ministry with Jesus. He witnessed miracles that shattered his own paradigm of what was really possible with God. He watched firsthand as blind eyes saw their first sights, deaf ears heard their first words, and the crippled took their first steps. He experienced the high of walking on water and the low of denying the man whom he loved more than anything.

Jesus prophetically warns the young follower that "truly, truly" there will come a day "when you grow old, you will stretch out your hands and someone else will gird you, and bring you where you do not wish to go. Follow Me!"

Though the words penetrate Simon Peter's mind, they do not pierce his heart. He doesn't want them to. Who would? Peter looks anywhere and everywhere for an escape. He finds one among the impromptu breakfast crowd. "Lord, and what about this man?" he asks.

"If I want him to remain until I come, what is that to you?" Jesus asks pointedly.

Then Jesus echoes the command, "You follow Me!"

Through that passage, God was speaking and anchoring me in the truth that above all else the greatest calling on my life was not my marital status or ministry but simply to follow him. My calling is to press my face into the shoulder blades of Jesus so that wherever he leads I will go.

You follow me.

Those words have become a holy reverberation in my soul.

That's often what happens when God speaks. The sacred echo reverberates inside of us long after the words are spoken.

Though that morning was the first time God spoke those words to me, it was far from the last.

You follow me.

That saying has become a sacred echo, an ongoing reminder from God of my simple calling. Years later, those are probably three of the most common words that reverberate in my heart from God.

Shortly after "You follow me" came alive in Scripture, I remember experiencing God's echo while I was jogging one evening at a local high school track. A few friends from the Bible college and I were committed to getting some much needed exercise.

As soon as our sneakers touched the track, one of my friends zipped off. A long-distance runner at heart, I took a much slower, steady approach. I was lapped within the first few minutes. Like an undesirable birthday spanking, the lapping didn't seem to have an end. The second friend graciously started out alongside me at a pace I like to call "wogging," my own home-grown blend of walking and jogging. After a lap and a half, he confessed that the slow pace actually caused him more pain than running a faster pace. He embarked on a stop-and-go series of sprints around the field. Meanwhile, in one corner of the track, a stranger was training for a specific track event. He was bounding and sprinting and running all within a confined area. The person seemed to be playing a game in which he alone knew the rules.

As I ran, the burning in my chest increased with each lap, as if spicy jalapenos were dancing in my lungs, but I pressed on, encouraged by the words of Paul that faith was like a race. As I continued around the track, something interesting happened. The guy in the corner, training in his own unusual and distracting way, disappeared. My friend who liked to sprint grew tired or bored after a few laps and decided to camp out on the bleachers. And my Speedy Gonzales friend, well, he grew tired after about twenty minutes.

Reflecting on the experience, my mind was drawn back to the echo,

You follow Me.

Don't be distracted by what others are doing. Don't worry about the speed, productivity, or efficiency of others. Don't be concerned with people who look like they're running in circles. Stay the course. They have their lane and you have yours. You need to follow me.

Such experiential moments of hearing God's voice are often the most difficult for me to recognize. I cannot imagine how many times God has wanted to speak to me about an encounter, experience, or exchange, but I don't have eyes to see or ears to hear. I don't pause long enough to ponder or pray. It's easy to point fingers at those in the New Testament who encountered Jesus but failed to recognize him as the Messiah. But I can't help but ask, *Am I any different? Are any of us any different?*

If God does not initiate and if God does not reveal, do any of us really have a chance of recognizing him, his voice, his echo? I think not—which speaks all the more to God's goodness and love and diligence in pursuing a relationship with us. Like the calling of the first disciples, he approaches each of us differently in ways we can understand. Maybe that's one reason he's so creative in his approach.

Though God was faithfully anchoring me in the truth that I was called and created to follow him, I continued to have doubts and distractions. Though I had internal peace for a few months that semester at Bible college, storm clouds eventually rolled in. Choppy waters surfaced. Doubts. Insecurities. Fears. I found myself questioning again, but God faithfully answered by reminding me of the lesson to follow him and reinforcing it again and again within my spirit.

My friends and I eventually realized that jogging at night near the inner city at night was neither the safest nor wisest of endeavors, so several of us decided to join a nearby gym with an outdoor pool. Donning a blue, one-piece Speedo, goggles, and a tight cap, I discovered swimming as a fusion of physical and spiritual exercise. Following the thick black line on the bottom of the pool, I steadily prayed for different people and situations with each passing lap.

One particular day, I noticed something oddly familiar in the encompassing underwater scene. In the lane next to me, a woman began swimming laps as quickly as she could. She sprinted from end to end, lapping my slow pace. She didn't last long. The swimmer in the next lane was even swifter but had to stop after each lap to rest. In the corner of the pool, I couldn't help but notice a woman in a floating device with a tennis racket. As she floated upright, she practiced swinging at an imaginary ball in the water. Training intensely, she was one of the strangest water sights I've ever seen.

In that moment, the Holy Spirit again connected the dots in my life, reminding me of the revelation at the track several months before, the echo of John 21.

You follow me.

Stop being distracted by the people in the lanes next to you. They have their lanes and you have yours. Keep your eyes focused on me, for only then can I open your eyes to things that you cannot see otherwise.

Though years have passed since my first encounter with the words,

You follow Me,

God continues to echo them throughout my life.

That's one reason I find spending time in Scripture so important. The Bible is not to be seen as a single volume as much as
a rich library for God's children. As I spend time in his Word,
studying the people, places, and passages, I expand the
resources that the Holy Spirit can draw from in my life. When
I feel completely out of control and begin to doubt that God
has any control, the Holy Spirit impregnates my mind with the
truth from Jeremiah 29:11 that indeed, God doesn't just have
a plan for me but a future too. When I am tempted to hold
a grudge against someone and allow the anger to get the
best of my heart, mind, and mouth, Ephesians 4:26 flashes a
basic life principle: Don't wait—forgive today. And when I feel
empty on the inside, a million miles from God, I remember the
simple invitation of John 10:10 that Jesus came that we may
have life and have it to the full. And when my faith is tattered
and I find myself doubting and questioning everything, I am
reminded of the simple truth: You follow me.

Last night we had dinner with a longtime friend, and the conversation circled to the issue of calling and ministry. Our friend
used to be the pastor of one of the largest, fastest growing
churches in the country before he was dismissed due to a

moral lapse. Though years have passed since the news of his dismissal exploded like a bombshell in the church, city, and life of this young leader, he is still in the process of recovery and restoration. He probably always will be. Because of what he's been through—the good, the bad, and the heinous—I listen extra closely to his observations and insights because he speaks not just as one who knows a truth but as one who has paid the price to own it.

When I asked him about any projects that he was working on, he mentioned a book proposal on the idea of calling versus ministry. "Your calling never changes, Margaret," he said. "But your ministry, well, that can change every five minutes. The problem is that all too often we sacrifice our calling for the sake of the ministry. The ministry becomes so important, so central, that we lose the most important thing."

His words still linger in my mind, bringing me back to those days at the Bible college. I see the names of those men and women on my prayer list, and I believe that many of them truly heard a specific calling from God at a young age. Today it's a joy to watch them serving him with their unique talents and gifts. Why didn't God speak to me about any future man or ministry? Maybe I wasn't ready. Maybe I couldn't handle it. Or maybe, in his grace and mercy he simply wanted to anchor me, like Simon Peter, in the truth that the calling to follow Jesus and our response to that call are all that matters.

As Leif and I travel, I'm amazed at how many churches are all too ready to jump on the next spiritual bandwagon. Starry-eyed from the numerical growth of particular congregations, church leaders are often quick to grab onto what they perceive as the latest Miracle-Gro tactics and snap-together programs.

Recently, we were with a church on the East Coast, and one of the leaders began sharing some of the struggles of pastoring a congregation in a rural environment. "It's hard to translate some of the things that edgier churches are doing into our congregation," he confessed. "In an effort to be sensitive to the landscape of our community, I have to be careful in what elements we add to our services. I love hearing what God's doing in other churches, but being here makes me feel insulated and behind the times."

"It's got to be hard," I conceded. "But don't forget the insulation is also your protection. You're not called to be the next so-and-so church. Though these institutions offer insightful best practices and helpful techniques, at the end of the day, you are called to follow Jesus right here, right now, right in this community with these people. You are called to be true to your own DNA and the way God has wired you. You are designed not only to reach these people but also to live and be among them. Don't be distracted. Remember that God can do great things through those who are slow, steady, and faithful. Your calling is simply to follow him."

As the words left my lips, I realized how far I had come since those days in Bible college. The words God spoke to me so many years earlier were not just in my mind but in my heart. They were becoming a wellspring of hope and encouragement to others. Even to this day, I am grateful for the steady reminder:

Remember, Margaret. You follow me.

.006 if you don't wear your crown

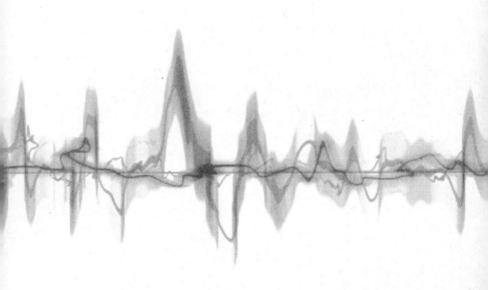

Tenacity is always inspiring. Reflecting on the life of my friend Shana, whose name is included on my prayer list, I find my faith reenergized. Five minutes with her reminds me of the behemoth size, power, and goodness of God without even mentioning his name. Some people pray as if their life depends on it; others live as if their prayers depend on it. Shana has mastered the art of both.

Like so many college graduates, I decided to move back in with mom and dad after earning a diploma. Shortly after returning to my hometown of Steamboat Springs, Colorado, I met Shana. She had moved from Denver to what we call "The Boat" and promptly joined a local church. The postmodern ski town was largely unchurched, and when Shana discovered there were only two other unmarried young adults in the congregation, she decided to do something. She rounded up the handful of believers and began praying for others to move to our snowy town. Within a few years, the group swelled to more than fifty, and we all stood in wonder at what God had done.

But that was only the beginning.

Shana is always vocal about her two great loves: making movies and caring for orphans in Africa. Each year she'd celebrate her love for film by hosting a formal Oscar party. I can still remember the year when Shana encouraged us to dress up for the event—my girlfriends and I donned brides-maid's dresses (the ones you promise the bride you'll wear again but usually never do). We ate fancy hors d'oeuvres and applauded when Shana gave her imaginary thank-you speech to the Academy—which, of course, included all of her Steamboat friends.

One spring I remember stumbling on a program for screen-writers in Hollywood called ActOne and encouraging Shana to apply. She overnighted her application. The acceptance letter became the catalyst for her move to Los Angeles to pursue her dream of making movies. When the course was completed, Shana launched Sodium Entertainment and began building a solid reputation in the film industry. To date, she's released two feature films.

Though consumed by the bright lights and blistering pace of life in Hollywood, Shana's heart still ached for Africa. She put together a film crew, raised money for equipment and supplies, and traveled to some of the worst humanitarian disasters in Africa. After the trip, she ended up returning to Uganda where she founded a nonprofit, grassroots organi-zation known as Come Let's Dance, designed to empower

African youth to initiate social and economic transformation in their communities. Come Let's Dance is reaching out to the orphans and widows in the slums and those dying of AIDS, ensuring they get the housing, food, and education they need. In addition, they sponsor micro-businesses including a taxi service and journal-making business in order to contribute to a self-sustaining local economy.

More recently, Shana's passion for film and Africa have fused; she's currently putting the finishing touches on her Africa documentary. I've watched Shana's life for almost a decade now, and her latest exploits are always a cliff-hanger resting on the hope that once again God will save the day. And he does—time and time again. Somehow Shana has managed to start her own entertainment company, film several movies, and launch a significant ministry with less than $1,000 to her name at any given time.

Some of my favorite Shana stories are the ones of God's just-in-the-nick-of-time provision. On countless occasions, she's been completely out of money, walked to her car, and found an envelope ripe with cash—the exact amount she needed down to the penny—waiting inside. Recently, she was back in the United States raising awareness and support for Come Let's Dance, when her tooth began to ache. She knew she needed to see a dentist, but she didn't have the money. The pain got so bad, she picked up the Yellow Pages and went to the first dentist's office who could get her in. The dentist examined her and announced that she needed a root canal. She closed her eyes, imagining the size of the bill and all the money she didn't have. While poking around in her mouth, the dentist began talking to her (in one of life's universally awkward moments). Shana began sharing about her community development project in Africa. The dentist wanted to know exactly where she was working in Uganda. He was delighted to discover that the village where Come Let's Dance is based was the exact same village he had grown up in. When she went to pay the bill, the balance was zero—it had been taken care of by the doctor.

Just watching Shana's life provides countless snapshots of faith in action and what it looks like to answer the call, *You follow me.* If God can do so much through one woman pursuing the passions of her heart and the calling on her life, then what could he do with me?

As I pray for Shana, I can't help but think about how God has seamlessly ordered my steps. Nearly a dozen years ago, I spent a summer working as an intern at a small Christian publication in Florida. I was fresh out of college and wanted to get some experience in publishing. By the end of the internship, I knew I loved writing. I also knew I wasn't built for a cubicle. I spent several months overseas attempting to be a missionary, only to discover that wasn't the life for me. That's when I decided to return to my hometown.

I spent several months praying about what to do with my life, and without hearing a peep from God, I asked myself, *If I could do anything with my life, and if time and money were not factors, what would I want to do?* I knew my answer instantly. I wanted to write. I sent out a handful of published samples and asked editors if I could write the reviews in the back of their magazines. I knew that if I could win an editor's confidence with the smallest publishable piece, then I could work my way up. Over the next five years, I progressed from reviews to news stories to feature stories to cover stories. In 2001, I published my first book. Since then, I've written more than a dozen books and Bible studies. I've spoken at national conferences, megachurches, and women's retreats. Yet despite everything, this path, this calling, this whatever-you-want-to-label-it remains one of the things that I wrestle with God the most about, because it hasn't been an easy path.

I've wanted to quit more times than I can count. I've wanted to give up, walk away, cry "uncle." Not just during the first six years, when I worked two to three side jobs to pursue my passion, but even over the last six years, when I've seen doors of opportunity swing wide open. In my writing and teaching, I feel like a Sherpa helping people ascend higher in their relationship with God. It's just that some days I get tired. Some days I get lost. Some days I want to return to base camp. And some days I want to quit.

God knows this. I tell him regularly. Every time I say, *I'm done*, he somehow renews my vision, my hope, my tenacity. Sometimes it's through an aptly timed email, "I just felt led to write you and tell you not to give up." Sometimes it's through a sermon or chance conversation. Sometimes it's through a scriptural reminder.

Still I wrestle with God. *What is this thing you're calling me to? I don't understand. Even if I did understand, it's still hard because I haven't seen it done before. The mountain feels steep, treacherous, and scary. God, can't we go back down yet?*

Last fall, I think God grew impatient with my second-guessing, my doubts, my insecurities. I remember a statement that flooded my mind, pressing firmly against my spirit:

If you don't wear this crown, I will give it to someone else.

I knew that in the Bible God would use anyone who was willing — even the unlikely apostle Paul. But was God really asking this of me? I cannot express the weightiness of those words inside my being. The density and heaviness of the rebuke was unfamiliar. I wasn't sure: was this God or my own imagination? I asked God to reveal himself to me, and I went to the place I hold as my standard: Scripture.

I began to research the crowns mentioned throughout the Bible and I was caught off guard by the description of the crown that Jesus wore: thorns twisted together. The wooden, prickly frame was a far cry from anything of a celebrated prince or king. The crown I felt God was calling me to don was one of surrender, service, and sacrifice.

When I stumbled on Revelation 3:11, I felt humbled, yet confident that God was dealing with some deeper heart issues. The verse simply says, "Hold on to what you have, so that no one will take your crown" (NIV).

Though the verse was written to a community of believers, I felt as if God was speaking directly to me. I knew that God was asking me to pursue the passion he had placed in my heart. If I was not willing to respond to the unique vocational calling he had given me, he would find someone else. If I was not willing to climb the mountain, God would find another Sherpa.

Still the idea made me a little uneasy. Would God take something away and give it to someone else? I thumbed through my Bible looking for a place where such an idea is even mentioned. I found it in an unlikely place: the parable of the talents. In this classic story of Matthew 25, Jesus describes the tale of three servants who are given various amounts of talents to invest. One servant is given five talents, while another servant is given two talents. Both make risky investments yet double their money. The third servant is given a single talent. Rather than risk what he's been given, he takes an über-conservative approach and buries it.

While the wise investing servants are richly rewarded by the master, the foolish servant is called "wicked" and "lazy." Then, the master instructs, "Take away the talent from him, and give it to the one who has the ten talents."

I realized that God was challenging me not to bury my talents. I'd love to say that once I recognized the core issue of surrender and service that God was pinpointing in my life, I immediately said, "Yes, Lord! I will pursue the passion you've placed in my heart. I will run hard and long and serve you with everything I've got." I didn't. For weeks, I grappled with the issue. God was asking me to commit everything and let go of all my what-if-this-doesn't-work-out backup plans, and I wasn't sure I wanted to hand them over.

If you don't wear this crown, I will give it to someone else.

The words churned in my soul. Though I first interpreted the statement as an ultimatum, I eventually came to understand it as an invitation. In a poignant way, God was saying,

I want to be glorified in you and through you.

I made you for this.

But if you will not allow me to be glorified in you, I will find someone else.

I am humbled to admit I withheld my decision, choosing instead to continue wrestling with God and myself. Is God really

still looking for men and women who will fully yield themselves to him? And when he finds them, what can he do in and
through them to glorify himself?

About a month later I went on a spiritual retreat with some
girlfriends, who like Shana, were making a difference in the
world. We had a lot of great conversations about the purpose
of our lives that weekend. Though there wasn't a particular
moment I can point to, I remember that at the end of that
weekend, I finally said yes to God. *I will wear your crown. I will
pursue the passion you've placed in my heart. I want to glorify
you with everything you've given me.*

Now I'd love to tell you that in that moment everything
changed, that in the following weeks, I saw my writing and
teaching blossom to new levels, doors of opportunity fling
open, and greenbacks fall from heaven. But that didn't
happen.

Instead, I simply sensed a new level of peace and understanding with God. Somehow I felt closer to him, like a child who
places her forehead against her father's chest.

Though more than a year has passed, I continue to reflect on
the words.

If you don't wear this crown, I will give it to someone else.

I don't think the work God began is finished, but I have seen

subtle shifts. The surrender that began in my heart is beginning to manifest itself in my life. I find myself using the phrase
"all-in" to describe my work. I'm not holding back anymore. I
can't remember the last time I wanted to quit. And I'm seeing more tangible fruit. Over the last few months, people
have been making decisions to follow Jesus when I teach. I'm
intrigued that people are coming to know Christ without a formal invitation. And this phenomenon has brought me to a new
realization; namely, that God doesn't want me to work for him
out of a sense of obligation, but out of a sense of gratitude.
While the difference is subtle, the implications are significant.
Recently, I was reading a book when the following words
popped off the page: "When we work with God instead of for
God, our sweat creates an intimacy. In fact, it becomes an act
of adoration and worship."

I see that demonstrated consistently in my friend Shana, and I
quietly pray this day that it may be seen in me as well.

As I reflect on the work God has been doing over the last year,
I stand in awe. I still don't know all the details of where God
is leading me, but more than ever I want to follow him there.
I want to join God in the work he is doing. I want to wear the
crown he has given and glorify him with all that is within me.
And I want to be able to throw the crown of my life before the
throne along with the elders and join the chorus, "Worthy are
You, our Lord and our God, to receive glory and honor and
power." Now that is a heavenly echo I don't want to miss.

.007 surrender

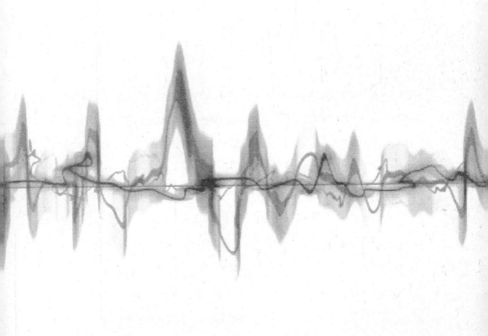

Bella was reticent, slow to give an answer, and rightly so. After not seeing her for several years, I was in her home in West Virginia, drinking out of her hand-washed, thick-lipped white ceramic coffee mug, asking her if she wanted to surrender her life to Jesus.

She had every reason to hesitate before giving an answer.

Our friendship had blossomed our freshman year of college in North Carolina when our social circles crossed. Bright-eyed, with a contagious smile, she could put the fun back into any function. On several occasions, we escaped the drudgery of homework and dorm life by retreating to her family lake house in West Virginia with a caravan of friends. We'd stay up until the early morning talking about anything and everything, then sleep past noon, wake up, and do it again. At least once every getaway, we challenged each other to run the ten-mile loop around the lake. Afterward, we'd lay on the floor of the living room, hot, sticky, exhausted, wondering why we just did that to ourselves.

Over the four years we knew each other in college, Bella had noticed a shift in my life. My faith was coming alive—not as a blaring siren, but through more subtle, unmistakable expressions. On a few occasions, we discussed spiritual matters and God, but nothing much ever came of those conversations— or so I thought.

After exchanging only a handful of phone calls and emails in the five years since college graduation, it was just chance that I visited her hometown during an epic cross-country road trip. I had finished a year in Florida at a Bible college and was once again returning to Colorado—a state that I just can't get away from as hard as I try. Rather than drive directly home, I decided to visit friends along the east coast before veering west. A few hours away by car, I surprised her with a call. We spent the evening laughing, reminiscing, and catching up on all that life had delivered on our doorsteps.

As the evening progressed, the conversation naturally veered toward spiritual matters. She asked what I believed about God. As the words rolled off my lips, I was immersed in self-doubt. Reciting the story of Jesus' death, resurrection, and imminent return, I felt as if I was delivering some fantastical piece of fiction rather than the foundation of my faith. *How could I ever believe this myself, let alone try to convince someone else?*

"You really believe that?" she asked.

"I do," I replied, secretly wondering if she could feel the vibrations of doubt in my soul.

Bella began sharing how faith—particularly Christianity—had always intrigued her. Though she hadn't grown up in a religious home, she noted a series of people she respected and appreciated, intelligent people, embracing Christianity and living accordingly. Now she wanted to believe too.

Time suddenly stood still. Taking a breath for emotional balance, I suggested, "Becoming a Christian begins with a simple prayer asking God to make himself real to you and then handing your life over to him. Faith begins with surrendering your life to God."

That's when Bella looked reticent and spoke something I will never forget:

"If I prayed with you right now, I would be doing it for you, not for me."

I looked down at the empty ceramic coffee cup, grateful for such rare honesty, thankful she did not pledge that which she would not keep.

More than seven years have passed since that evening in West Virginia. Bella and I have long lost touch. She has no idea that I think of her often, let alone pray for her regularly. When I was creating my prayer list, Bella was one of the names that haunted me. She's been there ever since.

As I lift her name to the Father once again, I ask God to make himself so real to her that she can't deny his presence. I pray that she will make the decision to follow God when her heart is ready and not a day before. I have a hunch she's the kind of person who, when she finally makes the commitment, won't bail—no matter what may come.

While praying for Bella, my mind begins to wander. I know one of God's great desires is for a relationship with Bella, but I can't help but wonder, *What does God want from me?* Now that I have a relationship with God is there more that he wants from me? One word impregnates my mind:

Surrender.

In prayer, my defenses go up. After all, God has already spoken to me about following him and wearing my crown. *God, aren't we done with this area? Can't we just move on?*

Yet the prayers for Bella further illuminate the issue of *surrender* in my own heart and life. I can sense that God wants to go deeper, peeling back the layers of my soul like a steamed artichoke knowing that at the center it's all about the heart. I begin to reflect on how many false-positive prayers I pray to God—things I say but really don't mean. All too often, after giving something to God—through prayer or verbal assent— I find myself taking it back. Well-meaning prayers like *God, take my life, my future, my everything* are followed by thoughts of everything-Margaret. Like a tug-of-war match with the Creator of the universe, my soul cries out, *It's all about you God, except when it's about me.*

The questions begin to surface: *What am I still holding back? What does it look like to fully surrender?*

Secretly I wonder, *Do I even have what it takes?*

Prayer is an altar for surrender, a place we go to hand everything over to God. Nowhere is this more clearly demonstrated than in the garden of Gethsemane when Jesus cries out not once but twice that his Father's will be done.

Prayer is the place where we hand things over to God on the deepest of levels, in our hearts, where he alone can see the exchange. Only after we surrender things to God on the inside can we truly hand them over externally.

As the word *surrender* echoes in my heart, I am reminded of the would-be disciple who asked Jesus for permission to first go and bury his father before following the rabbi. Jesus' response, "Follow Me, and allow the dead to bury their own dead" seems cold and rigid. But only recently did I realize the scandalous question the man was asking.

Like the unforgettable scene from the classic Monty Python film, the dad was "not dead yet!" If he had been, the son would have been sitting *shiv'a*, an intense Jewish custom of mourning based on Genesis 50:10. In essence, some interpreters believe the man was asking if he could go home, live in the comfort of family and community, wait for his father's death, collect the inheritance, and then become a disciple of Jesus. He wasn't concerned about following Jesus as much as fulfilling his personal agenda.

I want to be angry with the young man's question except that I find myself echoing the same sentiments. Instead of following God in the now, I take pause, wondering whether obedience to God is optional. *God, do I really have to get involved? God, how much time is this going to take? God, since I slept in, is there any chance we could reschedule?*

Yet surrender means giving over everything—including the micro-things. Recently I've been experiencing one of those seasons where God is reminding me that submitting to him means avoiding the shortcuts. The voice echoes throughout everyday life.

Surrender.

Take more time with this person.

Be extra generous in your gift.

Be completely honest with them.

Love your enemies, yes, even that one.

Just last week, I was about to press "send," turning in an article for a magazine when I felt impressed,

Read it one more time.

I found several errors. Though an editor would have caught them, I felt God gently reminding me, "Slow down, take your time, do it right."

Surrender means it's not just about getting things done, but *how* you get them done that matters. When Jesus speaks of walking two miles instead of one and giving your coat instead of just your shirt, he's saying that surrender takes many forms—everything including your schedule, your possessions, and, of course, your heart. Surrender asks us to hand over not just what we have but who we are to God.

All too often surrender makes me wonder what God wants to take away. I'm tempted to think morbid thoughts, like *What if God takes my best friend and husband, Leif? Would I be able to survive? Or what if God takes our house, our health, or even our puppy?* Then I remember that such incidents are not as much surrender as they are stripping. Surrender means willingly giving something over, while stripping is having something taken away. True surrender is not something that happens to you; it is something you willingly do.

One of the places I find surrender taking place is on that page at the back of my Bible. As I lift up each name, whether it's

Bella or any of the others, I see faces of people who I have so much invested in and who have invested so much in me. I see people who I've had the privilege of sharing all the bumps and beauty of life with for years. I see friends who I care deeply about and those who I've only met a few times but who have managed to capture my heart. Sometimes when I pray, I find myself asking God for what I want for them above what he wants for them. Instead of handing each person over to God through my prayers, I cling to them tightly, afraid of what God might do or, worse, leave undone.

In God's grace, he gently reminds me to surrender them to him in prayer. He has their very best interests in mind. He loves them more than I ever will. His ways are higher than my own. When I pray from a surrendered perspective, my prayers begin to shift from my personal wishes to his will being done. Instead of getting something from God, I find myself wanting to give to him in adoration, praise, and thanksgiving. Instead of ending prayer on empty, I find myself filled with the presence of God.

Whether in prayer or daily life, surrendering to God exposes a paradoxical truth: No matter what we give up, we are given so much more. Jesus goes so far as to promise that whoever leaves "brothers or sisters or mother or father or children or farms"—in essence, those who give up their earthly roots to be planted in an eternal kingdom—will not only receive a hundred times more now but even more than that in the age to come. And if you read the fine print, the promise also guarantees persecution.

That's where surrender gets messy. Given that surrender requires wholeheartedly giving myself to God (no matter what the consequence), what if bad things come, or worse, what if nothing comes? A few years ago, I stumbled upon a book on Christian leaders and missionaries, many of whom filled multiple pages with their accomplishments and work. Yet I only remember one entry: a missionary who lived in the southern tip of Africa for more than three decades without seeing a single convert. He was the only known person proclaiming the good news in that region for all those years.

With no measurable results, why did God place him there? Where was his hundred-fold? As many questions as I might have about the situation, the missionary must have had more. God heard every last prayer of this saint, yet still kept him there.

Despite their inherent beauty, such portraits of the surrendered life aren't always easy to look at. Something about them makes us wonder, "What if that was me?"

Over the years as a journalist, I have had the privilege of interviewing hundreds of people. A handful are quasi-famous, the rest largely unknown. Let's just say that while I've never met an A-list actor, I can still perk up a tepid dinner conversation with some less-than-subtle name dropping, like "I once interviewed Mr. T."

As a journalist, the best part about the job is that you're given a free pass to ask a person absolutely anything, poking around in the recesses of their life, their experiences, and even their soul. You never know what you will discover along the way. Once in a while, someone will say something unforgettable.

My interview with Steve Saint was one of those interviews. Steve is the son of Nate Saint. In 1956, his father, along with four other missionaries, Jim Elliot, Roger Youderian, Ed McCully, and Peter Fleming, made a historic journey to meet the Aucas or "naked savages" in the jungles of Ecuador. With an outrageous homicide rate, the tribe was famous for the habitual killing of anyone and everyone — especially their own people. After dropping gifts and supplies, the five young men felt they had established a strong rapport. Bathed in prayer, they flew into a remote site to meet the tribe.

Steve Saint was only five years old when he heard the news that his father and the other missionaries had been killed by the tribesmen. Five days later, a ground crew recovered the bodies, which had been pierced by spears. With gripping accounts in *Reader's Digest* and *Life*, the news quickly spread through the secular press.

In an unforgettable story of love and perseverance, Nate Saint's sister, Rachel Saint, and Elisabeth Elliot, widow of Jim Elliot, moved into the rainforest to live with the tribe. Eventually many of the tribesmen in the contact group converted to Christianity, including those who had killed the missionaries. Instead of hating or fearing the Aucas (who now call themselves the Waodani), Steve grew up loving the tribe and forming a lifelong relationship with them.

I was caught off guard by Steve's faith-filled candor during a phone interview when he said, "I don't think God allowed my dad and his friends to be killed. I think He orchestrated it with five men that gave their lives to Him. Bad things don't come from God, but sometimes they seem bad. The blood of the martyrs is the seed of the church. Most people don't want to give God liberty to use their lives that way, because we call it tragic. Most think that it's okay to go with God's program as long as it fits their program. But I finally decided that I wanted God to write the story, because I know that it will come out best in the end that way."

Steve was right—God was writing an amazing story in the jungles of Ecuador—the kind that makes a journalist's mouth water. But that's not what haunted me.

Somewhere in our phone conversation, Steve began drifting from the story of Waodani to his own story, his own losses. The previous year, Steve and his wife had lost their daughter,

Stephanie, to a sudden cerebral hemorrhage less than nine hours after she had returned from a yearlong mission trip.

"I saw her lying there, looking normal," he said, as if he was still beside his daughter's hospital bed, "I really believed that if I would just pray and beg the Lord to restore her, he would have."

In that single confession, the conversation transitioned from interview to intimate as Steve described the most difficult moment any father can face. I sat silently, sensing the weight of the moment.

"But I couldn't bring myself to do it," Steve continued, "because I've been through things ... that seem tragic, God uses (them) for His own purposes."

"Wait a moment," I said, hesitant that I had misunderstood the story. "You mean you sat at your dying daughter's bedside with the full faith that God would heal your daughter if you prayed, but (still desired) God's will over your own?"

"Yes."

. . . . .

. . . . .

"Are you still there?" he asked.

"Yeah," I whispered, baffled by what to say next. We sat

together for the longest moment in silence. I had heard count-less people say that God works all things together for good, but few people owned that statement like Steve Saint. He had paid the price with his father and now his daughter.

"Does the loss of your daughter still hurt?" I asked gently, wondering if I had crossed that invisible boundary that every journalist respects and fears.

"My heart has a huge hole blown in it and even grandbabies don't fill the hole—they just help heal around the edges," he answered.

Before I ended the interview, Steve gently reminded me of a quote from Jim Elliot he felt was appropriate for the article: "He is no fool who gives what he cannot keep to gain what he cannot lose."

Surrender.

I still can't wrap my head around it, but on that day with Steve Saint I felt like for the first time I was beginning to wrap my heart around it. I don't know if God intended to heal Steve's daughter, and I'm not convinced his decision not to pray was the best response. Yet, it powerfully illustrates that the nature of surrender is not external; it is internal. Surrender is not an exploit—something we do—as much as a renovation—some-thing that is done in us.

True surrender is not a single action but a posture in life, yielding ourselves—our whole selves—to God. Breathtaking opportunities for surrender will surface throughout our lives, but grabbing hold of them begins below the surface, in the deep places of the soul where God is already preparing us not just for those moments but for himself.

As I pray for Bella this day, I can still see the look of reticence in her eyes. I'm grateful for it, thankful that she didn't verbally surrender that which her heart did not want to give. I pray God will continue making himself real to her, bringing her to a place where she is ready to yield.

Surrender.

May the work God is doing in her life be done in my own.

.008 take care of my people

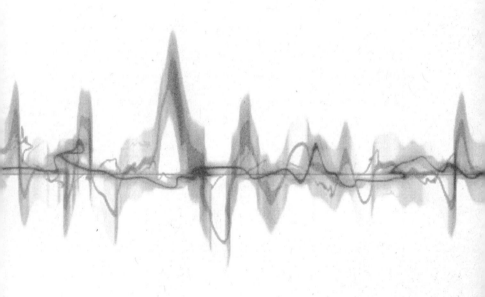

"Why don't we do this more often?" Maggie asked.

A fair question. Leif and I were spending a week speaking and hanging out at a church in the heartland of Pennsylvania, participating in an Inside Out project together—a day when the members of a local community of faith tangibly make a difference in the lives of those in the surrounding area. We raked leaves and washed windows for the local elderly, single moms, and disabled.

Full of energy and warmth, Maggie immediately made me feel at ease. As someone who processes verbally, Maggie liked to talk. That was a good thing, because I liked to listen.

As we raked, she suddenly stopped and said, "I am so glad that I came today, because I almost didn't."

I waited for her to explain.

"I was supposed to work today at the Olive Garden," she said. "It's the best shift, but I really wanted to come out and serve too. I didn't know if financially I could afford to give up the shift because of rent coming up, but I prayed about it and felt like I should. So now I'm here, and I am so glad."

"I'm glad too!" I affirmed.

"I know I want to make a difference, and I know God wants me to make a difference and serve others, but I also have financial needs. How do you know the balance?" she asked.

I bit my lower lip, gently reminding myself that Maggie processed ideas verbally. She needed to discover the answer herself. We continued raking and tossing soggy leaves into stinky trash cans, chatting for the rest of the afternoon.

That night we attended church together, and the pastor spoke on caring for the poor and those in need. Maggie couldn't shake the question, *Will you live with less so others can live with more?* After the gathering, Maggie pulled me aside and said that she finally realized the source of her quandary: her apartment. She shared a sweet crib with her roommate. The sizable rent forced her to work extra hours and avoid taking any days off. As she sat in the church service, she felt the invitation to transformation, to surrender her life more fully to God.

Through a random conversation the next day, she learned that one of the members of her faith community was buying a house and could provide more affordable living for Maggie and her roommate—lowering their financial stress levels and increasing their ability to give more not just of their resources but of themselves.

I recently caught up with Maggie. She was in the process of downsizing, donating the extra stuff that had accumulated all too quickly in the nooks and crannies of her apartment. Though Maggie and her roommate are planning to move out soon, Maggie says she can't shake the sense of something bigger that she needs to be doing. She's been dialoguing with a local leader who is trying to organize a group of young adults to build intentional community with the mission to serve in a particular neighborhood. Maggie is going to take some time off of work tomorrow to make space to pray and think. Where will she live? What will happen next?

I don't know. Neither does Maggie.

God is clearly at work in her life. Through her own quiet times of prayer and meditation, circumstance, church, and community, she's hearing God's voice echoing. Consistent themes of downsizing, giving, and serving others combine with an unmistakable sense of peace and expectation that can only come from God. And it's clear that the work he's doing is about more than just a new address or less stuff. His work goes deeper into her heart, soul, spirit, and mind. God is transforming the way she sees herself, others, the world, and those in need. She's finding verses in the Bible come alive in a whole new way. Like a physical reverberation, the sacred echo has movement in her life. Just listening to her story makes me want to ask, *God, what is truly important to you?*

The discoveries in Maggie's life remind me of the transformation taking place in my own since I decided to surrender to God. Lately, the sacred echo I have been hearing in my heart is simply this:

Take care of my people.

The echo is drawn from that foundational passage in my life: John 21. After breakfast with his disciples, Simon Peter becomes the center of Jesus' attention. Turning to the young follower, Jesus asks the same question three times with slight variation.

Simon, son of John, do you love Me more than these?

Simon, son of John, do you love Me?

Do you love Me?

To each question, Simon Peter persists.

Yes, Lord; You know that I love You.

Yes, Lord; You know that I love You.

Lord, You know all things; You know that I love You.

Jesus closes each exchange with similar instructions.

Tend My lambs.

Shepherd My sheep.

Tend My sheep.

The repetitive nature of the exchange is unmistakable. Jesus persists in his question of love. Both the simplicity of the question and the persistence with which Jesus asked made Peter question, doubt, and feel slightly misplaced. Peter is forced to fasten himself to a foundational truth, "Lord, You know all things."

Jesus gently but intentionally reminds Peter that true love translates pragmatically into caring for the saints. Tend the lambs. Shepherd and tend the sheep. In other words, take care of the young ones, but diligently lead, guide, and care for those who are older as well. For Simon Peter, the fruit of truly loving God is outward-focused, missional living.

Take care of my people.

Though those words are slightly different than the ones Jesus used in his exchange with Peter, they have become a steady reminder to care for God's people. Along with this recognition that I am called to love and care for others who are less fortunate, God is opening my eyes to the reality that the poor cannot always be identified by their material lack. The Bible describes a people who have acquired wealth to the level that they do not need a single thing. Yet God exposes the poverty of the über-rich: "You do not know that you are wretched and miserable and poor and blind and naked."

Indeed, I need to take care of God's people everywhere.

While it's often easy to measure material poverty by what someone does or does not have, it can be much more difficult to identify or measure relational poverty and the pain and loss that come from being alone or without life-giving relationships. I often think that real connection between people is more valuable than gold, and life without such connections is the poorest of all.

This first came alive in my heart shortly after my husband, Leif, and I moved to Juneau, Alaska. We were new to the area, something biblical writers like to call *aliens*. Before we moved, we had asked three different pastors from three different denominations in a neighboring town for church recommendations. They all named the same church. We attended, fully committed to discover what God had for us.

Leif and I made a conscious decision to study the DNA of the community in an effort to discover where we could best serve. We also needed time to get settled. We were busy buying our first home, and Leif was starting a new job, as well as going back to school to finish a degree in business management. We faithfully attended church each week. There was only one problem: no one talked to us. Okay, a few people here and there said hello, but despite our efforts to reach out, we received little response.

After four months, I was frustrated and discouraged. While Leif stayed behind after a service in another attempt to build relationships, I retreated to the car. *Why is it so hard for us to make friends here? Why won't anyone talk to us? What is it, God?* Big, wet, hot tears rolled down my cheeks. I finally looked up from the steering wheel and noticed several other young adults leaving the church. I watched as they each got into their vehicles and drove away in different directions. I knew in that moment that I wasn't the only one who felt this way.

That's when I first knew we had to do something, anything, to help others who felt as alienated as we did. Recognizing our own relational poverty helped fuel our desire to reach out to others. We began inviting people to our home after church, serving lunch, and hosting spiritual discussions using the NOOMA video series. More than a dozen joined, and the comment that we heard again and again was the same: *We needed this—why didn't we start this sooner?* Out of that little group, relationships sprouted, prayers were answered, and my own heart cry for community had been met. Now that doesn't mean that it was always easy. Hosting, cleaning, and cooking, because few of the members had a home where everyone could meet, eventually led to exhaustion and burnout for me. Building community is never easy. Yet it still remains one of the most rewarding things Leif and I have done and is one small tangible way we could care for God's people.

As our budding community grew, I began making a connection point with what I saw in times of study. The words of James came alive in my heart: "Pure and undefiled religion in the sight of our God and Father is this: to visit orphans and widows in their distress, and to keep oneself unstained by the world."

In the ancient world, the orphans, widows, and aliens lived in a cultural context in which they were more likely to be in financial need, but they were also more likely to be in relational need. Orphans, widows, and aliens, by their very nature, have all experienced relational loss. They have been separated from those they love. God tells us not only to give them food and financial support, but also to come alongside them and build relationships. He instructs us to invite them onto our land to glean and invite them into our feasts to eat. These are not people to be marginalized and set aside, but to be acknowledged, included, and appreciated. In moving to a new city in Alaska, Leif and I had become aliens. Suddenly, this passage was not about someone else—it was about us and it opened our eyes to the need to care for others.

Like a catchy chorus from an alternative rock song,

Take care of my people

reverberates in my life, and I can't quite shake it.

I was becoming more sensitive to the needs of all kinds of people. While living in Alaska, I had to travel to New York City for a small medical procedure. Recognizing that I had some extra time in the Big Apple, I made a list of places I wanted to visit including the hipster tourist hot spots like Times Square, Broadway, and MoMA. I also wanted to spend a day with the Sisters of Charity. I called several times before a sister finally answered. In a broken, hard-to-understand German accent, the woman gave me the address and told me to show up the next morning at nine o'clock.

The mission was located on a back street south of Harlem, and as I approached the address I suddenly felt extremely self-conscious of being a white, middle-class woman walking alone in an unfamiliar city. Nearing the entrance to the run-down building, I felt slightly intimidated by the dozen homeless men sitting around the front door. One of the men asked, "You here to help?"

I nodded.

"Let her through," he announced.

I felt a wave of relief that I had met his approval. Once inside, a small, zippy nun smiled and said, "God sent you here!"

"I guess you could say that," I answered hesitantly.

"Where are you from?" she asked.

"Alaska," I answered.

"God sent you all the way from Alaska to be with us. The other volunteers who were scheduled couldn't make it today. He sent you."

Without missing a beat, she pointed toward stacks of cups instructing that every setting needed a glass. Work began, and before I knew what happened, two nuns and I had set tables, served food, cleared dishes, handed out to-go bags, and washed dishes for forty homeless men. For the nuns, every action was efficient and deliberate; they ran a tight ship and though I felt like a novice, they welcomed my extra hands. I didn't catch my breath until we were preparing for the next meal.

That's when we finally stopped moving—or at least our feet did. Another volunteer from the community popped in, and the four of us sorted through the bags of donated vegetables, salvaging pieces of potato, carrot, and onion for an afternoon stew. As we sliced and diced, I fell prey to my journalist nature and asked dozens of questions. We talked about God and simplicity and the richness that comes from serving the poor. The two nuns had long since left their families, their homes, and all their worldly possessions. With long hours and significant duties, the life they had chosen was not easy, but as my time in that tiny kitchen revealed, their lives were abounding with real joy—the kind no amount of money can buy.

As I was leaving the Sisters later that day, the same woman who greeted me early in the morning smiled widely and reminded me, "God sent you all the way from Alaska to be with us today."

"I think you're right," I agreed, knowing that I had received far more than I ever could have contributed.

When I think about that unforgettable day, I can still feel the reverberation of this echo in my life:

Take care of my people.

Slowly, God is opening my eyes to needs all around me. In Scripture, God revisits this issue of caring for the poor—an echo that repeats itself from Genesis to Revelation. The Bible acknowledges that the poor will always be part of society, but God takes on their cause. The Mosaic law of the Old Testament is filled with regulations to prevent and eliminate poverty. The poor were given the right to glean—to take produce from the unharvested edges of the fields, a portion of the tithes, and a daily wage. The law prevented permanent slavery by releasing Jewish bondsmen and women on the sabbatical and Jubilee years and forbade charging interest on loans. In one of his most tender acts, God made sure that the poor—the aliens, widows, and orphans—were all invited to the feasts.

Why is God so repetitive? Does he have an ax to grind? A soapbox to stand on? Or is there something more? Perhaps God is persistent because he wants his heart for the poor beating inside of us.

I'm reminded of my own coffee-stained prayer list in the back of my Bible and my steady petition: "Give me eyes to see people as you see them, ears to hear what you're speaking, a heart to love as you do, and hands to serve as you want to be served." My newfound awareness of poverty in all shapes and sizes is a direct answer to this prayer.

I asked the Lord, *show me more*. Soon after, I began studying the book of Luke with a new lens. I never realized that this particular gospel was a lush collection of teachings on finance and wealth. According to theologian Craig Blomberg, Luke addresses a slightly better-off Christian community with his gospel, thus leading to his emphasis on money. This is the book in which one man is told to sell everything and give it all to the poor, yet a few pages later we read a parable where servants are given money and rewarded based on their investments. This is the book where Zacchaeus, a tax collector who became wealthy through dishonest means, offers to give half his fortune to the poor and repay those he stole from. Instead of asking that the rest be given to the needy,

Jesus declares that salvation has come to Zacchaeus's house. Though Jesus was clearly anti-stockpiling and anti-waste, he was pro-generosity. He defended the woman who wiped his feet with her tears and expensive perfume. The Samaritan is applauded for giving money and personal service. Joseph of Arimathea provided the costly tomb in which Jesus was buried and Theophilus was most likely a wealthy, high ranking official who underwrote the publication of Luke's manuscript.

Such a wide variety of responses to wealth in one gospel reminds us that there's not a single prescription for handling money. Though selling all and giving to the poor may be the *magnum opus* for a few, it is clearly not for all. Just as Jesus extended a warm embrace to the poor, he also welcomed the rich, asking all to serve one another in generosity of spirit. Why? Because in the process of looking after those in need, something transformational happens. We begin to open our eyes to the world around us rather than just focusing on ourselves. We begin to recognize those in need in our neighborhoods and community and decide to cross that invisible threshold of awareness and actually get involved.

At times, that means writing big checks and handing over wads of cash to those in need, but it also means delivering bags of groceries, shoveling snowy walkways, mowing out-of-control lawns, volunteering to babysit, and serving in the countless tiny ways that make a big difference. Sometimes I think the best gift that can be given to someone in need is a long afternoon together on a shady porch with a pitcher of iced tea.

I saw this play out during a retreat on Lake Lanier in Georgia. While enjoying an afternoon of tubing on the lake, we learned the story of two mansions that sat across from each other on opposite sides of the lake. Both were owned by Christian couples. One of the couples prayed and asked God what they should do with their home. He instructed them to keep the home, enjoy it, and use it to bless as many people as they could. The other couple prayed and asked God what they should do with their home. They felt the Lord say, "Sell it—this home has a grip on you. Use the proceeds for the ministry I've called you to."

Sitting in the boat, I looked at both gorgeous homes in humble awe of God's grace, wisdom, and mercy. Both couples had cried out in prayer. They offered their own questions to God asking for his leading, direction, and wisdom. God faithfully answered, but his answer was not the same. The path he was leading each couple down was unique. The work he wanted to do in and through their lives was different.

Through my friend Jonathan, I recently got an update on the two Christian couples. The couple who faithfully kept and used their home to bless and serve others eventually felt like the Lord was telling them to sell it. Guess who bought it?

The man from the other mansion! After ten years in hands-on ministry, he felt led to move back to the lake.

God knows each of us intimately. He knows we each need something different depending on the season in our life. The buying and selling of the houses on Lake Lanier revealed that God was doing a deeper work in each person's life than they probably imagined.

That's the nature of the sacred echo. It's not just about hearing God's voice so we know what to do or leave undone, but so we may know God. The echo reverberates so that his words and his faithful persistent voice in our lives lead us closer to him. The realization that poverty is not a zip code is just the beginning of a deeper work God is doing in my life. It's an invitation to ask God, *Why is this so important to you?* and *Why should this be important to me?* It's an opportunity to share the richness of response with friends like Maggie and grow in our love of God together.

When I think about the sacred echo of Maggie's life which involves downsizing, sacrifice, and generosity, I recognize many parallels in our conversations with God. We both have a sense that he is at work in our lives. We both recognize that he is opening our eyes to Scripture. We both know that he is changing and shaping our perspective to see things just a bit more like he does, preparing us in greater ways to care for his people. And we both have a hunch that the conversations we're having with God are part of a greater conversation that is taking place across his kingdom.

The joy of listening to God's voice and taking care of his people cannot be contained.

Have you heard the sacred echo? May he take us deeper still.

.009 bring them to me

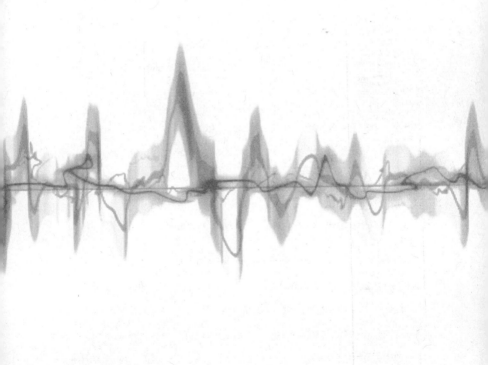

It was supposed to be a routine surgery. A small excess bone fragment from an injury years earlier was lodged in Kyle's shoulder and needed to be removed. An overnight stay in the hospital was recommended but not required. He'd be home soon—the minor medical nuisance gone—except for one detail: the surgeon was having an off day, and his scalpel nicked the edge of a nerve. For Kyle, that one cut sliced his life into a million irreparable pieces.

I saw it on his face when he was finally released from the hospital. He described the fiery challenge of painkillers which don't actually kill pain; they only take the edge off. The initial dosages were addictive, the withdrawals worse than the chronic pain they were designed to relieve.

Once home from the hospital, Kyle began to wrestle with the reality of a surgery gone bad. How do you forgive the doctor? Yourself? An irreparable situation? He was instructed not to lift anything over a few pounds to minimize further damage. That meant countless activities were off limits for Kyle, everything from helping his wife with housecleaning to carrying groceries to lifting up one of his two young sons to hug them. Living in

Alaska only compounded the difficulty of the situation because of the isolation and lack of quality medical care. Despite the pain, most days Kyle carried a sunny disposition. Things would get better.

They didn't. The battle with painkillers—the flimsy line between relief and addiction—was unrelenting. The needs of his spouse and children only compounded as they grew older. His wife was growing increasingly tired, their intimacy waning, the marriage slowly dissolving.

Life threw my friend Kyle one of its ugliest curve balls and as much as I wanted to save the day, all I could do was pray. In the most solemn of requests, I asked God to heal, restore, and renew. I prayed for God to do something, anything, to make the pain stop. On several occasions, I even fasted for my friend, begging God to say "enough," to do the impossible. *Please, oh God, please.*

That was three years ago.

Last spring, I learned that Kyle tried to take his own life. The attempted suicide shook his family and the Alaskan community but did nothing to alleviate the pain. As I pray for him this day, I want to scream a bloody four-letter word in frustration, anger, and disappointment on his behalf. Instead, I find the meager resolve to offer up a four-letter prayer, "Help."

Why doesn't God heal him? Sometimes I think more

scandalous questions revolve around the issue of healing than any other. God's arm is not too short, and yet somehow, somewhy he holds back—not just from Kyle but from millions of others. Doesn't God see? Doesn't God know? Doesn't God feel? Why doesn't he do something?

This question, this prayer, stirs in my heart. As I've wrestled with God, I've discovered four words that have been like a balm to my weary soul: *Bring them to me.*

I first discovered this echo while studying Mark's account of the boy possessed by a dark, cruel spirit. The demon tortured the child by throwing him to the ground, eventually leaving his body exhausted and as stiff as a board. The boy's father was desperate. He approached Jesus' disciples begging them to cast the spirit out, but the disciples' efforts did nothing to relieve the torment.

When Jesus heard the story, he exclaimed, "O unbelieving generation, how long shall I be with you? How long shall I put up with you? Bring him to Me!"

My eyes paused on the final four words. In this heart-wrenching story of suffering, Jesus' answer was simply,

Bring him to me.

Once the boy was brought to Jesus, he was dramatically set free.

In the ache I felt for my friend Kyle, I sensed God whispering,

Bring them to me.

At first the phrase seemed cryptic. What should I bring to you? Who should I bring to you? In the stillness of my soul I knew God was asking me to hand Kyle over to him in my heart and trust him.

Up to that point, I had been praying out of anger, frustration, and disappointment, but I hadn't been admitting any of those feelings. God used the account in Mark to remind me that there's no pain, torment, or suffering that have escaped his notice, and none are beyond his redeeming power. While Jesus healed men and women brought to him, I know that I may not see such instant results. I may have to wait in faith. But as I wait, I am reminded that I don't need to wait alone. I can bring them to God.

This sacred echo brings a holy hush to my soul. I am reminded that some things are beyond understanding, but God does not leave me there. He invites me to run back to him.

Bring them to me.

Those words take the focus off the pain, the horror, and the loss and invite me to shift my focus back to Jesus. He is the one I am to turn to and rely on. After all, he is the only one strong enough to carry any of us through. When Jesus is at the forefront of my mind and heart, I am in a better place to pray, to serve, and to be a voice of healing and life.

In those moments when the heaviness of a situation and the pain that comes with living in a fallen world become too much, God echoes,

Bring them to me.

As a result, I've been noticing that I'm getting bolder in the questions, doubts, and pain I take to God in prayer. More and more, my spiritual spunk can't be contained. And I'm finding that the writers of Psalms, Ecclesiastes, Lamentations, and Job also took their toughest questions, their heaviest weights, to God. They asked the most jarring of questions, probed the darkest of issues, and confessed their hurts and betrayals without ready apology.

While Jeremiah complains about God's unfairness, Habakkuk goes so far as to accuse God of being deaf. They place all their brutal honesty under the umbrella of prayer. If prayer was a safe place for those men and women to get brutishly honest with God, then shouldn't it still be safe for us today?

Bring them to me.

That God allows, invites, and even welcomes such blistering outbursts of passion reveals the depth of his desire for relationship. God doesn't want a surface, shallow friendship.

He doesn't want to be mere acquaintances. He wants to sort through the muck and mire that comes with any meaningful relationship.

In Jewish tradition, questioning is not just acceptable but encouraged. If you were to visit a Jewish synagogue, you'd discover the Rabbi asking countless questions, some of which sound scandalous. Throughout the Bible, God asks questions of people as people ask questions of God. In the Gospels, Jesus asks his own Father if the cup of suffering can be taken from him (Mark 14:36), and in the book of Job, Satan and God exchange questions—none of which have ready-made answers.

Questioning is also one of the crucial ingredients of an ancient practice known as Jewish midrash. This method of study invites us to wrestle with God through his word. In Hebrew, midrash means *to search out*. Midrash asks the reader to look at difficult Scriptures, ask questions, and try to make sense of them before God. Midrash invites us to become venturesome with the Bible and to trade in a surface understanding of Scripture for a deeper grasp of a passage's meaning and, along the way, to discover more of God and his ways. The questioning, the searching out, becomes a foundation for growth and discovery.

Why does questioning make us so nervous? I recently had a pastor tell me, "Sometimes I find myself wondering what people would say if they knew all that rolled through my mind. When I experience doubts, would my congregation be comforted to know that their pastor deals with these questions? Or would they be horrified?"

I am convinced that all of us have at least one scandalous question. Some have dozens, even hundreds. Odds are you have a few of your own. Stop and think for a moment:

If you could ask God anything, what would you ask?

Don't pull any punches. What would you ask? What have you been secretly longing to ask him for years?

Though such honest heart questions sometimes startle us, I have discovered that God does not pull back, turn aside, or duck from such wonderment.

Bring them to me.

Not only does he invite such questions; he even asks a few of his own. All too often the answers he provides, if any at all, aren't the ones we anticipate, expect, or can even fathom.

I'm confronted with this every time I pray. Sometimes I'm able to keep my questions and doubts at bay, breezing down the list like aisles of the neighborhood corner market. When I stop to reflect, I see rows of hopes and hurts, dreams and disappointments, a strange weave of pleasure and pain in response to the prayers. Yet I keep coming back, accepting the invitation again and again, not just because I'm asked or instructed, but because something in my heart longs for resolve. Deep down inside, I really want God to be the one who provides it, the one who makes sense out of this nonsensical world.

Many of my toughest questions for God revolve around the issue of healing. Maybe it's because so many of those listed in the back of my Bible remain sick after years of prayer. I can't help but think about the multitude of those who were sick, blind, and unable to walk lying by a pool near one of Jerusalem's sheep gates—their bodies weathered not just by the sun but the hardness of life. Of the hundreds of bodies resting near the pool, the gospel of John records Jesus addressing only one. Knowing that this particular man had been sick for thirty-eight years, Jesus asks, "Do you wish to get well?" (John 5:6). Though the man does not address the query directly, Jesus instructs him to get up, take his mat, and begin walking. In a moment of miracle, the man is instantly healed.

What about the others? What about their lives? Their days? The long years they continued waiting near the sheep gate, sun beating down, hope slowly fading? What about them?

I'm not the only one who aches with such questions. I know so many who are sick and waiting for healing, not just for their bodies but for what's transpired in their souls. Anyone who has faced the horrors of medical malpractice or physical malfunction knows that sickness is not just about what happens to a body but what happens to a life. The ripple effects touch the deepest recesses; nothing is immune. Sickness affects how we feel about ourselves, our relationships, and our world—inadvertently altering our activities, abilities, and our attitudes.

And in the midst of so much pain and torment, the invitation remains the same:

Bring them to me.

I want to respond to the invitation, but my heart is guarded. Though I've seen God heal, I'm still afraid of the disappointment if he doesn't. I've known people who were told they'd never walk again but who now jog every day. I've known people who were advised they'd never survive cancer who are living vibrant lives. And I've known people with deadly diseases who have miraculously survived.

I was once part of a church missions trip to host a conference in Honduras. At each session, our team prayed for anyone who came forward and hundreds of people flooded the front of the meeting area. A longtime family friend, Elizabeth, and I prayed for a woman who had a painful tumor in her neck. We placed our hands gently near the tumor and prayed for several minutes. The woman was obviously moved by the experience. I asked her in Spanish if she felt anything, and she said "No me duele." The pain was gone. When we felt the area where the tumor had been, it felt soft like something had been removed. Elizabeth and I looked at each other in disbelief. Then we began poking and prodding her to confirm the healing. I must have asked the woman a dozen times in Spanish, "Now are you sure there's no more pain? Are you really sure?"

Neither Elizabeth nor I could believe what had happened. We still laugh with joy that we got to be a part of what God was doing. We know beyond a shadow of a doubt that her healing had nothing to do with us. Our level of faith was low, yet God healed her anyway.

When we shared the story with our team that evening, a long-time American missionary to the area told of praying for a local man whose leg was too short. As he prayed for the man, he actually watched his leg grow longer. At the time, the missionary didn't really believe that God healed like that—he was just responding to the man's request for prayer.

A few years later, I was part of a small team going door to door to talk about and show the love of Jesus in a low-income area of Monroe, Louisiana. I'll never forget one particular house. The paint on the home was flaking like dried skin after a sunburn, and the screen door was more door than screen. When we knocked, a child answered, and we asked if we could talk to her mom. "She's in da kitchen," she offered.

Unsure of how to proceed, I gingerly opened the door. Several people lounged in the living room entranced by the television. "May we come in?" I asked.

No one responded to our arrival. I nervously kept talking. One of the women nodded, and said, "Come on back."

Stepping into the cramped kitchen, a woman sat at a worn wooden table with her forehead pressed against her palms, eyes swollen from tears. Disconnected details poured from her lips. She had lost her son to a random gunshot. Bills were piling up, and she wasn't sure how she was going to stay afloat financially.

"Can we pray for you?" one of the team members offered.

"That would be nice," she smiled. "Can you pray for my headache too? My head is just killing me right here."

We gathered around the woman, gently placing our hands on her arms and back. I came around the back side of her and placed my hands on her head, and each of us took a few moments to pray out loud for her loss, her finances, her health. We asked God to surround the house with protection and provision, to renew and restore. After several minutes, the woman grabbed both of my hands, turned around, and looked at my palms and then at me and said, "What you got—magnets in those hands?"

"Excuse me, ma'am?" I said.

"You must have magnets in those hands because my head-ache is gone. I could feel it leave as you prayed."

"We all prayed," I reminded her.

"Yeah, but I felt it out of your hands," she said confidently.

"Well, my hands may have been the ones you felt, but God's hands are the ones that heal," I pushed back.

"Amen," she said.

We sat around the table for some time, talking about life, listening to stories of her son. Before we left, we asked if there was anything we could do, and she said, "I really could use some food."

An hour or so later we returned to her home with paper bags of fresh groceries. But what she gave to us—allowing us into her life at a pivotal moment—was far greater than anything we gave to her.

Why did God choose to heal a woman's headache that day? Why did we get to be a part of it? And why did she grab my hands? I didn't have a particularly large dollop of faith that day. If truth be told, I don't think my prayers were really the ones God answered. But somehow, somewhy, he did some-thing and that woman knew it. And somehow, somewhy, on a whole lot of other days he doesn't do anything we can see—no matter how much we believe, hope, negotiate, or beg.

Why?

Why is my friend Michael still limited to a wheelchair despite my countless prayers? Why does my friend Tracey suffer from migraines despite more than a decade of prayers? Why does my friend Jenna still live with crippling arthritis despite my prayer, fasting, and begging God?

Why does my friend Rachel have to watch her husband suffer from an injury caused by a doctor, an injury that his parents then didn't properly care for? Though the injury affects his everyday life, there's nothing Rachel can do, so she struggles with anger toward the negligence of the doctor and her in-laws.

Why did my friend Grace's father die suddenly from a heart attack? An avid runner and swimmer, he had even completed a triathlon. Grace's mom, a nurse, never thought for a moment he had any heart problems let alone heart disease. With the sickness undetected, he died one month before his son graduated from high school and one month before he would have graduated from a master's program.

Grace quotes Romans 8:28, saying that "we know that God causes all things to work together for good to those who love

God, to those who are called according to His purpose." But she admits that she began hating God because she couldn't see how taking her dad's life could possibly be good. While time with a counselor and friends who have loved her through the loss have helped, she still wonders why. Why didn't her dad ever get to meet her husband face-to-face? Why didn't her dad get to walk her down the aisle? Why won't her dad ever meet his own grandchildren? She says she doesn't expect to know any answers to these and other questions until she goes to heaven. Maybe then, she adds, it won't matter anymore.

As I pray, I hear the echo,

Bring them to me.

Slowly I find myself bringing everything to him—even the toughest of questions, the most difficult of situations.

A few months ago we were caught off guard by a call. Our friends from Alaska were at a local hospital in Denver praying for their child's recovery. The story we heard on the phone was nightmarish.

The friends had left their one-year-old son with a trusted babysitter. While playing, the child managed to pull over a play chest. The wooden structure hit him in the forehead. The babysitter saw the child lying quietly and thought he was simply resting. She left him there for hours. When she finally went to move him, she realized that something was deeply wrong. The doctors confirmed the tragedy: the child was paralyzed from the forehead down. He was sent to one of the best children's hospitals in the country, which just happened to be in Denver where we now live.

When we heard the news, Leif and I jumped in the car and raced to the hospital. I didn't know what to expect—of our friends or the child. I had never visited a children's hospital before and pulling into the parking lot, I instantly recognized this as someplace special, someplace sacred. Walking through the lobby, I saw children no more than three feet tall with their hair stripped by chemotherapy. I watched as one young boy ran circular laps, breathing unusually hard and loudly. The joy of the movement was in his eyes and face but not in his lungs. The atmosphere of the hospital carried an unmistakable tenderness, because you knew everyone was dealing with something difficult. You just didn't know what.

As we rode the elevator up to our friend's hospital room, I found myself sucking back the tears. I widened my eyes to increase the surface tension lest a tear fall. They fell anyway. I was having an emotional reaction to the children's hospital, which, for me in that moment, was a portrait of living in a fallen world stripped of innocence, perfection, and health. Approaching our friends' hospital room, I wiped away the tears stuffing my damp hands in my pockets to hide the moisture.

I put on the happiest-yet-appropriate-for-the-moment face I could muster. Our friends had experienced so much loss and hardship, and I didn't know how to respond. Leif and I gently asked questions and listened. We were encouraged by the news that since the accident the boy had gained slight movement in one of his legs. The parents had hope for recovery. Hooked on a ventilator and feeding tube, the child was unable to eat, drink, or move his arms. When he screamed because of pain, discomfort, or hunger, nothing came out because of the breathing tube. Listening to the silence broke my heart.

As I stood at this toddler's bedside, I heard God whisper something to me that I have never forgotten:

This happens to some of my children.

In the painful stillness, I knew what God was saying to my heart. Some awful things happen as a result of living in an imperfect, fallen world. Some are the result of our choices or the choices of others. Some things happen with no real rhyme or reason. Though nothing is beyond hope, God alone is the source of that hope. I wanted to tackle God with a million *Why* questions. I had them lined up and ready, but something about that phrase echoing in my soul reminded me that maybe the *Why* questions weren't the best questions to be asking in the moment. Maybe rather than explaining things I couldn't possibly comprehend, God simply wanted me to know that we were not alone in that hospital room. God was with us. He alone was our source of comfort.

I found my heart filled with compassion not just for the young boy but for so many others who have experienced unexplainable loss, pain, and tragedy.

Though it's been several months since our evening in the hospital, we are still praying for the boy's full miraculous recovery. We serve that kind of God. But I still find the words echoing in my heart:

This happens to some of my children; you may not understand, so bring them to me.

Those words do not make me question God's love or goodness. They do not make me doubt his power to redeem, heal, and restore. Rather, they fill me with compassion that can only be given from above.

My intellect tells me that this particular sacred echo raises too many theological questions without providing any answers. That makes me uncomfortable. Then, I begin to realize that the echo isn't speaking to my mind as much as to my heart. The words are a reminder that I never really know what's in someone's past or future. I may never really know what tragedy has befallen them or what's to come. I may never really know what causes someone's pain.

But I can still be a source of healing. I can still love. I can still pray. And I can still listen for the sacred echoes, because during times of unexplainable loss and pain, the words of God are what get me through. In those moments when everything is unfamiliar and unclear, I find strength in the foundational Scriptures of my faith and cling to these sacred echoes I know to be true until the storm ends. In the process, I discover the depths of God's love, redemption, and hope that I would not know otherwise.

Leif and I have a dear friend named James. At the age of six, he was molested by a priest. More than five decades, four marriages, and three addictions later, he has never really recovered. The bitterness and anger have eaten away at his soul leaving him with a vinegary personality. James is easy to make mad, but nearly impossible to convince to forgive.

Despite his sour disposition, Leif and I love James. We can't really explain it. He says the most awful things and it's like we love him even more. I don't know where that kind of love comes from or why we've been given such love in this particular relationship. But James is a well-worn name on my prayer list. After years of prayer, things only seem to get worse.

As I ask God a hundred questions of "Why," I am hushed by the reminder that this happens to some of God's children. And I am reminded once again that God loves James more than Leif or I ever will. Though I'll never understand the horrible loss or trauma that has scarred his life, the sacred echo reminds me that it's safe to trust God with James. He knows what happened and he will not readily let go.

This happens to some of my children; you may not understand, so bring them to me.

Some things are just beyond earthly explanation or understanding, but in his bigheartedness, God did not leave me there.

Sometimes God heals; sometimes he does not. While we can point to factors that contribute to one or the other result, healing remains largely a mystery. Healing also remains a promise. I can't help but think of the vision John received while imprisoned on the island of Patmos: "Then he showed me a river of the water of life, clear as crystal, coming from the throne of God and of the Lamb, in the middle of its street. On either side of the river was the tree of life, bearing twelve kinds of fruit, yielding its fruit every month; and the leaves of the tree were for the healing of the nations."

That's the same river which promises to "make glad the city of God." I want to dive in and feel its cool waters spray across my face and bring everyone I know with me. After a playful swim together we will climb onto the shore. One by one we'll select a fruit. Tasting the tangy sweetness on our lips, each bite will bring the promise of life and health rather than sickness and death. Sitting under that glorious tree, each leaf will be a reminder that God has risen with the fullness of healing in his wings.

The healing promised is not just physical, but carries a more holistic meaning of "making whole." Deep down, that's the pang of my heart, maybe the ache of all of our hearts, *God— make us whole.* And maybe, just maybe, when I respond to the invitation,

Bring them to me,

I become a little more whole myself.

As I pray this day, I ask not just for healing, but for wholeness for Kyle and so many others—including myself—and I dream of the day that we will splash and play and swim together.

.010 you are not alone

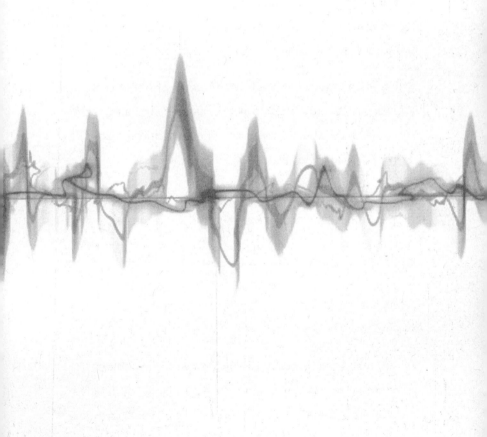

We recently visited with Sharon, a lovely woman in the South. She was a veteran believer who had weathered the storms and triumphs of living a life in relationship with God. Her warmth and hospitality were extraordinary and manifested themselves in a whopper of a peanut butter pie. I can still taste the sugary sweetness on my tongue when I think about it now.

Sitting in oversized barstools at the edge of her kitchen counter, we talked about cooking, life, ministry, and faith. When the topic shifted to prayer, she confidently said, "I've learned it is better not to ask God for anything."

The statement threw me, particularly from a longtime Christ follower. I looked at her quizzically. "If you don't ask for anything, then, what do you talk to God about when you pray?"

"Well, I ask God for things for other people but just not for myself," she clarified.

For years she had prayed specifically to God. With no visible reply, the disappointment had become too much. Heartbroken, she simply stopped asking. Throughout our

conversation she never named the prayers that went unanswered. She never named the first unanswered prayer or the
last specific prayer she prayed. I don't know the loss, the pain,
and the hurt she experienced in that silence. As she shared,
I couldn't shake the feeling that something inside of her had
died.

I felt sad.

I wanted to offer some peppy words of hope, some meaningful Scripture, some God-infused wisdom that would bring her
back to life, but I didn't have any. Sure, I could have conjured
something up, but in stillness I just prayed.

God, how do we respond when all we hear is silence?

Though I heard nothing in reply, I am still praying for her
today.

While many sounds can hurt our ears, I think silence is the
most painful because it can hurt our hearts. In the silence, we
are tempted to fill in the blanks in our life, our future, and our
relationship with God. And that's dangerous. In the silence,
we are tempted with doubt and fear, and, worst of all, we may
resort to the godlessness that sprouts from trying to make
things happen on our own. Meanwhile, we're prone to make
agreements that are not founded in truth. Thoughts like *God
is not good, God is not trustworthy*, and *God does not care*
sink into our souls. Like a barbed hook, they don't leave easily.

Once the wound is inflicted and the hook ensnared, the infection of disappointment and disillusionment sets in. Before we know what has happened, anger surfaces, followed by guilt. In an effort to handle the guilt, anger, disillusionment, and disappointment, we draw a line. After all, lines are simple. Lines are straightforward. Lines make us feel safe.

If left unchecked, those lines become boundaries, barriers of self-protection from God:

I won't ask God for anything he won't give.

I won't ask God for anything too specific.

I won't ask God for anything too personal. Too meaningful. Too miraculous.

That way, neither God nor I have to cross the line. The line of self-protection works perfectly, except for one little problem: whenever we draw a line with God it's as if something inside of us dies.

I recognized the death in my friend's eyes because I have seen it in my own.

A few years ago, I was assaulted by a mysterious illness. I was becoming violently ill after eating. I could eat a meal one day and be fine and eat the exact same meal the next and become radically sick. Sometimes the response mirrored food poisoning. Other times the sickness imitated the flu, leaving me ill for five or more days. With neither rhyme nor reason to the reactions, I visited various doctors and hospitals and endured less-than-pleasant medical tests and even surgery.

Several years have passed since the first gut-wrenching attack, and I'm grateful that even though medical science has never been able to resolve the illness, I have learned how to manage it on my own through proper diet, stress management, medication, and rest. Today, I'm far more able to recognize the foods that will make me ill, including wheat and full-fat dairy, and avoid them. On a more lighthearted note, I've discovered that eating fat-free frozen yogurt before getting on an airplane is not the best way to love my neighbor as myself.

For the first year of the illness, everyone was highly concerned, including me. Some of the stomach attacks were so violent and unbearably painful that I wondered, *Am I going to die?* As the incidents continued, I was relieved to discover that if I just held on long enough the painful episodes passed.

From time to time, I had the energy to ask God why. *Why me? Why now? Why this?* I never heard a reply—only a sense of peace that was enough to let me know that no matter what happened it was going to be okay. If God wore a polo shirt, then I felt like I was resting in his front pocket, dark but safe.

As the months passed, the sickness began to wear on my soul. Though I still had a sense of peace, the silence was beginning to hurt my heart. Was God going to heal and restore? Was this new normal here to stay? In the silence, I grew despondent. The Bible says that hope deferred makes the heart sick. Without realizing it, I drew a line with God. I placed hope on one side of the line and myself safely on the other.

Leif noticed the change. He knew something was wrong beyond what was already wrong. In his Leifington (that's my pet name for him) way, he looked for ways to cheer me up. At the time, we were living in Alaska. One Sunday morning in the middle of winter, he kidnapped me and brought me to one of my favorite places: the glacier.

Before I moved to Alaska, I had never seen a glacier; but when we moved to Juneau, we had one just a few miles down the road from our house. When I first laid eyes on Mendenhall Glacier, the icy mass took my breath away. Scarred by boulders and deep crevasses, the frozen surface filled an entire valley. I never grew tired of visiting the glacier.

Bundled up, vanilla latte and hot chocolate in hand, we made our way across the frozen lake at the foot of Mendenhall Glacier and stood before the frigid mass in awe of its blue beauty. Though slightly frozen ourselves, we leisurely made our way home before heading to church. I loved that morning.

A few nights later, Leif woke up in the middle of the night. Startled, he grabbed me tightly.

"You're still here," he said, his voice trembling with fear.

"I'm here," I responded, shaken.

Leif had dreamed that we were walking on the lake at the glacier. Unexpectedly, the ice began to crack. He watched, horrified, as I fell into the frozen water. In desperation, he tried to pluck me out, but I was out of reach. There was nothing he could do.

"I'm fine. I'm here," I assured him, dismissing the dream. After all, we weren't planning another glacier outing anytime soon.

A few nights later Leif had the same dream again.

I found it mildly interesting in a he-sure-is-concerned-with-the-glacier way.

Then he dreamed the same dream a third time.

That's when he had my attention—or rather God had my attention. Leif is not a repetitive dreamer by nature. I couldn't help but wonder, *Was this a sacred echo? Was God trying to get our attention? If so, what was he trying to say?* As I prayed, I realized that the dream was a picture-perfect portrait of how I felt inside. Like cracking lake ice, the mysterious illness had caught me unaware. I had fallen into a hole that required all my energy just to survive. And in my heart, I had drawn a line with God. I had given up hope. That meant the people around me who wanted to love me, breathe life into me, and rescue me were just out of reach. I was pushing them away.

I began to recognize the seriousness of the situation. I began reaching out to others, asking for prayer and making every effort to reengage with friends instead of hiding and handling things on my own.

Around that time, I found a passage in Scripture that exposed my own heart. First Kings describes the wild adventures of Elijah the prophet. After an impressive showdown on the crest of Mount Carmel involving a handful of false prophets and enough fire to please any pyro, Elijah finds himself on the run again from the evil queen Jezebel. Afraid for his life, he narrowly escapes into the wilderness, where he bottoms out at an epic low. He wants to die.

The ice has cracked.

A single phrase of Elijah's prayer, "I have had enough, Lord" caught my attention. Those five words summed up everything I was feeling, everything I was afraid to give voice to. While I appreciated Elijah's honesty, I also identified with his exhaustion. Elijah was without hope. So was I. And I needed it more than anything to survive. Studying the rest of 1 Kings 19, I discovered that God did not leave Elijah alone. The prophet was about to get a wingman, Elisha.

Through that passage, God illuminated a powerful truth in my life:

You are not alone.

Through that realization, God erased the line I had drawn between him and me, hope and me. I was still in God's pocket, and I was not alone. I had a husband, friends, and a community who were ready to embrace me despite my brokenness, my sickness, and my lack of faith. For me, that was a turning point in the road to recovery, the path to healing God had intended all along. I was coming back to life. Though I still wrestle with this illness every day, my hope is back and I feel alive again.

You are not alone.

Of all the sacred echoes, this may well be one of the most powerful and liberating. The more you isolate yourself—whether from God, family, or friends—the more you die inside. That's why this sacred echo speaks life and hope into the darkest of situations and the most discouraged of souls—whether it's a southern woman's, Elijah's, or my own.

Often when people say that they don't hear from God and conversational intimacy is not part of their lives, a traceable line is etched in their past. Just this afternoon, I hung out with a college student at a local café. While bubbling with energy for snowboarding and her friends, Madison admitted that she had been struggling with her relationship with God.

I asked Madison how she best experienced and discovered God. She was quick to explain that God became real to her through her relationships, through other people. I gently prodded further into her spiritual life. Madison only cracked open her Bible about once a week. Whatever she read felt flat. Whenever she prayed, all she heard was silence. Meanwhile, her roommate was living the "perfect Christian" life, complete with daily reading, studying, praying, hearing, serving, doing, going and going and going. Though slightly annoyed with her ultra-disciplined roommate, who she was convinced was on the fast track to burnout, Madison knew there was still something very real going on between her roommate and God. The hunger stirred in her own heart.

Circling the wagons of conversation back to the issue of silence, I asked, "Do you ever ask God to speak to you?"

"No, I never thought to do that," she explained. "I just kind of assume he'll start talking."

"Why don't you ask?" I pressed.

Madison began to share the story of her uncle who had shot himself intentionally. When they found his body, he was still alive. Rushed to a hospital, Madison and her family pleaded with God for his life. They prayed fast and hard and specific.

They asked God to preserve his life. They asked God to make the suicide attempt a turning point in his life. They asked God to use this incident to help launch a ministry where he could bring hope and life to others who were hurting.

Within the hour, her uncle died.

Madison's relationship with God went silent.

I asked Madison if there were any lines that she had drawn with God on that fateful day. She nodded. I encouraged her to prayerfully erase the lines by inviting God into those areas to restore the truth of who he is in her heart. Give him full access. Welcome him into the conversation of her life. Most importantly, I reminded her,

You are not alone.

We all have prayers that go unanswered. We all experience disappointment with God.

My time with Madison makes me think that if left unchecked, the silence of unanswered prayer can take an enormous toll on the human soul. In the silence, we fill in the blanks with disappointment, rejection, loss, and pain. In a desire for self-preservation, we isolate ourselves from God and eventually others. We draw lines until our prayers begin to shrink. Smaller, more modest prayers become the agenda, the new norm, shielding us from exposure to disappointment, discouragement, and discontent. Yet deep down I know such efforts of self-protection only result in self-imprisonment— a self-constructed dungeon where the window of hope is too small for escape.

That's when I find hope in the story of Sarai, the wife of Abram. Like my mom, she was a childless woman and asked God for a child. Though my mom only had to wait eight years, Sarai had to wait much longer. And Sarai's wait was not easy. After all, if her husband was going to be the father of many nations, then she was supposed to be a mother. Yet decades passed with no child. In the silence, she drew a line between herself and God. She gave up hope. She decided to fill in the blanks herself. If God wasn't going to give her a child, then by golly, she could get one on her own.

She made the case to her husband, Abram, that if he slept with their servant, Hagar, they could extend the family line. He agreed. Almost as a side note, Genesis 16:2 adds, "And Abram listened to the voice of Sarai." Interestingly, the verse is an echo of an earlier exchange between Adam and Eve found in Genesis 3:17. Neither Abram nor Adam took the time to ask God about the matter, to listen to his voice.

The result of Sarai's self-sufficiency was Ishmael. Yet despite the family drama that ensued, God never left Abram and Sarai. He continued to pursue them. More than thirteen years later, God sent three men to Abram (now known as Abraham) and Sarai (now known as Sarah) to prophesy that Sarah was going to become pregnant. When she heard the news, she laughed. I don't think Sarah laughed because the words were funny. I think she laughed because she had long given up hope on God in this area of her life. The line she had drawn years earlier was still firmly in place.

The men challenged Sarah's laughter. "Is anything too difficult [or wonderful] for the Lord?" The words must have stung, because Sarah immediately recoiled, denying the laughter. One of the men called her on it, "But you did laugh." The line in Sarah's heart was exposed.

For me, this story is a welcome reminder that even when we draw lines with God, he does not draw them with us. He is committed to breaking us out of our imprisoned thinking and renewing our minds and hearts and spirits with the truth. God wants to set us free and often he will use others to do it.

My last summer in Alaska I discovered that my friend Emily, a beautiful woman full of laughter and life, was living in one of the darker cells of disappointment with God. She somehow convinced me to pick blueberries with her in the rain. She explained that the bushes were popping with juicy abundance and we couldn't afford to wait another moment. I put on my raincoat and hoped the baked rewards of my foodie friend were worth the soggy work.

We drove to a remote area to find a secret blueberry patch

someone had shared with Emily. Because she had never visited the field before, it wasn't long until we were lost, driving confusing mountain roads in search of fruity treasures.

"God, please help us find this blueberry patch," I prayed, the words flowing off my lips smoothly, effortlessly, without much thought.

"You can't pray to find a blueberry patch," Emily corrected.

"Really?" I asked, realizing the silliness of my prayer.

"God doesn't answer those kinds of prayers," Emily insisted.

"Maybe," I answered, "but at this point, God is the only one here who knows where this blueberry patch is—so we might as well ask him."

"But God has bigger things to worry about than our blueberry patch," she answered. "And he just doesn't answer prayers like that."

I could tell from her tone we weren't talking about blueberries.

"Why do you think that?" I asked gently.

She deflected but eventually began sharing the story of her mother. A few years before, her mom saved up enough money to retire. She purchased a house in a small community. One night a man broke into the home and brutally attacked and killed her. The man was arrested, and the trial went to court.

He was found guilty and sentenced to prison. Reflecting on the testimony in the courtroom, the judge described the event as, "The most gruesome crime he had ever seen during his time on the bench."

That's when Emily turned to me and said, "I know my mom. I know that she cried out to God to do something, anything, to stop the abuse in her final moments, and God didn't do anything. If God didn't answer then, why should we expect him to answer now about some blueberry patch?"

I sat in silence. The issue wasn't about berries or prayer but about God. How could he hear those cries and not respond? How could the God, whose arms are not too short refuse to extend? Where was God in her mom's greatest moment of need? Why the silence?

I don't have any answers. I don't know why God answers some prayers and not others—no matter how hard or how long we pray—or why God answers selfish prayers, because we've all prayed them, but leaves a woman alone to die a horrific death.

I ache to know. While driving those back roads with Emily, I felt her pain, not just the anguish of loss and anger and a million unanswerable questions, but the pain of the prison she now found herself in. The line she had drawn between herself and God had become a deep, dark moat. Emily knew God could answer some prayers, but unsure of the response, she found it safer to pray as few as possible.

We sat together, embracing the silence which always seems like a welcome friend after such intimate confessions. In that moment which was the raw footage of her life, I reached out to her. And I prayed that for a brief moment she would experience the simple transforming truth that she was not alone.

When we finally found the blueberry patch, I spent some time in prayer, not just for her but myself. Emily wasn't the only one who had drawn lines with God. While she took out her anger on the small prayers like those for blueberry patches, I took them out on the big prayers by not praying them at all. Her honesty revealed some of the darker crevices of my own soul. I still have areas where I'm afraid to trust God, where I've been disappointed in the past, where I still need his healing and restoration. I am now asking God, *Show me the lines I've drawn with you. I don't want to be isolated from you or anyone else.*

Slowly God is answering that prayer. He is committed to erasing the lines I've knowingly or unknowingly drawn in my life. At times, we're all tempted to fill in the blanks with things that are not true. Yet God invites us out of such imprisoned thinking. He wants to erase the lines, even the hidden ones, and bring redemption and restoration. No place is off limits for God. No hurt, pain, or disappointment is beyond his healing power. Even when he must—for reasons beyond my understanding—say no and let the fallenness of our world crumble in on me, he invites me to pray. Even when my prayers are seemingly too big for my britches or too small for his concern, he invites me to pray. And even when my prayers are met with nothing but silence, he asks me to keep praying.

With every prayer my window to the world grows a shade bigger, the rays of light shining in become brighter, and before I know it I find that I'm not living in a prison cell but rather as God intended. Prayer might not change things, but it will change my perspective of things. Prayer might not change the past, but inevitably, it changes my present.

I don't know the specific lines you may have drawn with God. I don't know how you've chosen to fill in the blanks in the past. But I do know that *you are not alone* and I am confident that like my friend Sharon, God is committed to breaking you out of any boxy prayer life and setting you free to commune with him.

Are you ready to erase the lines?

God is.

awakened

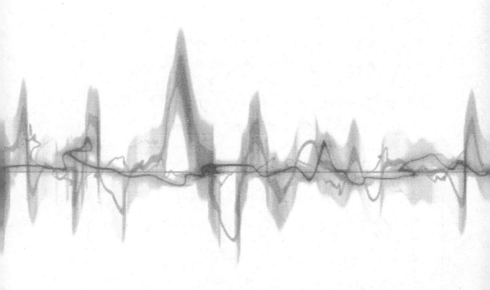

Final words should always be savored. That's why I find the instructions of Jesus in the account of Matthew so intriguing. He tells us to make disciples of all the nations, baptizing them into the name of the Father, the Son, and the Holy Spirit, teaching them to observe all things instructed. It saddens me that at times, this rich, powerful commission is reduced to nothing more than convincing someone to sign a prayer card, dunking them in water, and handing them a stack of self-help books.

Being a follower of Jesus is so much more. One of my favorite commentators says that a better translation of the phrase "baptizing" is actually "immersing." The literal meaning of this command carries significant implications. Christ was instructing us to go to the ends of the earth to *immerse* people into the reality of God, Jesus, and the Holy Spirit.

When you've truly been immersed into the God-reality, nothing stays the same—including you. That's one reason the sacred echo is so important to our spiritual lives. The sacred echo, the persistent voice of God, reminds us that he is passionately pursuing a relationship with us.

At times, I feel like Lucy from C. S. Lewis' *The Lion, The Witch and The Wardrobe*, running around, crying to anyone who will listen that it's real — it's real — this whole God thing is more real than any of us can imagine. The words you read in Scripture aren't just encouraging or inspiring. Those descriptions of heaven aren't just colorful phrases. Those teachings of Jesus aren't just good ideas or principles. They are real life, both now and to come.

The naked truth about "getting saved" is that becoming a follower of Jesus will not make you richer, skinnier, or more prosperous. It will cost you everything — more than you can imagine — as you pour your life into causes that no one else seems to care about. But the rewards, well, I'm gambling with everything I've got that they're worth it. Like Lucy, it's worth believing and bringing everyone I possibly can along for the adventure.

That's why I've put on my "be brave" T-shirt and shared some of the more intimate sacred echoes from my life. I believe that as we share the things we hear God speaking we can help fan the flames of spiritual awakening — not just in our own hearts but in the lives of those around us.

Recently, I asked my blogging friends, *What does God's voice sound like?*

The answers and adjectives were intriguing: Ambiguous. Assuring. Beautiful. Clear. Cool. Comforting.

Compassionate. Confident. Convicting. Demanding. Gentle. Infrequent. Intriguing. Peaceful. Rock solid. Scriptural. Stable. Still. True. Tantalizing. Unique. Unwavering.

My friends described God's voice as quiet yet dynamic. Though loud and startling as thunder, God's voice is also as soft as the sound of a feather falling. One friend compared God's voice to snowflakes falling in the glory of a majestic sunset. Yet at other times, God's voice is like an annoying alarm clock, buzzing that horrible sound which means it's time to make a choice, to do what our bones long for or what our spirit is called to.

When I asked the same community, *What has God been whispering to you?*, the answers glimmered like pearls:

You are my beloved.

My will is not your desire and your desire is not my will.

Receive me in the quiet moments.

This is that which will endure: greater love has no man than this, that he lay down his life for his friends.

My strength is made perfect in your weakness.

Let me shelter you.

Take care of my children.

Pay attention to those around you.

Love one another as I have loved you.

My hope and prayer is that this will not be the end of a conversation but the beginning of an endless conversation of what God is doing not just in your life but in the lives of so many who are just beginning to discover the reality of God. Some of the sacred echoes I've shared in this book still reverberate in my life every day:

I love you

sing it again

how long?

read it again

you follow me

if you don't wear your crown

surrender

take care of my people

bring them to me

you are not alone

The sacred echoes in your life are probably going to be slightly different than those you've read, because God reveals himself to each of us differently. When you find your mind awakened by a Scripture that won't let your heart go, know that there's a good chance God is speaking to you. Don't ignore it. Pay attention. Take the echo back to God in prayer. Be confident that he is leading you, guiding you, and revealing himself to you. And when you find a healthy community, celebrate what God is doing in your life by sharing your sacred echoes with others so that we can all grow in our relationship with God together.

I'd love to hear what God has been speaking to your heart. Please email me at margaret@margaretfeinberg.com.

reflection

three questions to consider with each reflection:

1. What concept, phrase, or story from the chapter was the most compelling to you?

2. What concept, phrase, or idea from the chapter did you disagree with?

3. What is the one thing that you want to take away with you and put into practice?

.000 exposed

- In what ways can you relate to Margaret's description of being a "yo-yo pray-er"?

- In what kinds of situations or moments is your prayer life most alive?

- What are some of the adjectives you'd use to describe your prayer life?

- What are some of the characteristics of your prayer life? What disciplines or practices help you connect with God?

- Many questions about prayer are asked throughout this introductory section. Which questions can you most relate to? What are some of your own questions about prayer?

- In the story of 1 Kings 19, God spoke to Elijah through a whisper. The Scripture clearly says the Lord was not in the wind, the earthquake, or the fire. If he was not in those things, then who was?

- Like an echo, God used the repetitive nature of the wind, earthquake, and fire to prepare Elijah for an encounter with himself. What kinds of things does God often use to get your attention?

- Has God ever spoken a sacred echo—a scripturally based message—to you? If so, describe.

holy reverberations

Read Luke 18:1–8.

- *Why do you think tenacity or persistence is so important in prayer?*

- *Jesus was specific in the details of this parable. The story is about a widow, an unjust judge, and a cry for justice. What are some lessons that can be drawn from the details of the story?*

- *How does reading this story affect the way you approach God in prayer? Your attitude? Your expectations?*

.001 i love you

- In what ways do you feel like you're "flying in the dark" when it comes to prayer?

- Have you ever taken the time to ask, "God, what's on your heart?" If so, what was the response?

- Have you ever felt like God has told you that he loves you in a way that was meaningful? If so, describe.

- Deep down inside, do you really believe that God loves you? Why or why not?

- Why is knowing and experiencing God's extravagant love so foundational for a faith journey?

- How does knowing and experiencing God's love change your posture in your relationship with him? On a piece of paper, draw a picture of the posture of someone who has experienced the love of God.

- Why do you think God is so repetitive in the things he speaks to us in the Bible and throughout life?

holy reverberations
Read Ephesians 3:17 – 19.

- *Why do you think Paul prayed this prayer?*

- *What does it mean to be "filled up to all the fullness of God"?*

- *Do you think that fullness is a one-time event or an ongoing experience? Explain.*

.002 sing it again

- What tends to distract you most during prayer?

- Do you ever use memorized prayers, a prayer journal, or a book of prayers? If so, how do these enhance your prayer life?

- When you think back on your faith journey is there anything specific you'd like God to "sing it, again!"? If so, explain.

- What passage of the Bible have you read a dozen or even a hundred times that always speaks hope and life into your spirit? Why is this passage so meaningful?

- If your prayer life were a style of music, what style would it be? If your prayer life were a song, what song would it be?

- Why do you pray if God already knows your request before the words leave your lips?

- How have you seen prayer tangibly change your life or the life of someone you love?

---

holy reverberations

Read Isaiah 43:1–5.

- What specific phrases catch your attention as you read this passage?

- What specific phrases are words of comfort and encouragement in your life right now?

- What do you think God is trying to communicate to the Israelites through this passage?

.003 how long?

- Why do you think waiting is such a fundamental part of our personal lives? Our spiritual lives?

- What are you currently waiting for?

- What is your most common response to the process of waiting?

- When was the last time you found yourself in-between? How did you respond?

- In what ways can waiting make you more like Christ?

- What can waiting accomplish in your life that speed cannot?

- Do you really think good things come to those who wait? Why or why not?

holy reverberations

Read Psalm 62:1–6 and Isaiah 40:30–31.

- *What is promised for those who hope and wait on God?*

- *In what ways have you seen these promises fulfilled in your own life?*

- *Describe a time when you waited for God's best and got it.*

.004 read it again

- What was your response to the first paragraph of this chapter? Did you notice the repetition? Were you bothered by it? Explain.

- How do you respond to the repetition of God in your life?

- Why is it important to take time not just to read Scripture, but to reflect on its meaning?

- What prevents you from taking more time to reflect, research, and pray as you study Scripture?

- In what specific way has God recently revealed himself as intimate and personal to you?

- What Scripture has recently captured your attention and led you to discover something new about God, yourself, or the Bible?

- Why do you think God is so committed to speaking to us through Scripture?

holy reverberations
Read John 1:35–51.

- *Make a list of each of the different ways Jesus revealed himself to the initial disciples.*

- *Why do you think Jesus took such varied approaches?*

- *Why do you think it's important to recognize the different ways in which Jesus reveals himself to his followers?*

.005 you follow me

- Have you ever experienced a micro or macro crisis of faith? What happened?

- Why do you think the foundational truths of Scripture are so important during those difficult times?

- The words "You follow me" became evident to Margaret in a variety of situations. Have you ever had a particular Scripture or passage follow you through life events? If so, describe.

- Why do you think it's important to anchor yourself in Scripture?

- What are some passages from the Bible that have been like spiritual anchors to you?

- What does God steadily remind you of?

---

holy reverberations

Read John 21.

- *What surprises you most about this chapter of the Bible?*

- *Why do you think Jesus was so specific in his dialogue with Peter?*

- *What do you think Jesus wanted to teach the disciples (and all of us) through the breakfast on the beach?*

.006 if you don't wear your crown

- Why do you think it's important to respond to the God-given passions of our hearts?

- What are some of the potential outcomes if we don't make ourselves available to be used by God?

- Have you ever been in a situation where you found it difficult to say "yes" to God? If so, describe.

- Have you ever said "no" to God? If so, what was the outcome?

- What do you think is the difference between working with God and working for God?

- Can you identify a deeper work that God has been doing in your life? If so, describe.

- What do you feel is the "crown" that God is calling you to wear?

---

holy reverberations
Read Matthew 25:14–30.

- *Which of the three servants do you most relate to? Why?*

- *Why do you think the master took the talent that had been buried and gave it to the man who had ten talents?*

- *Why is it important to use the gifts and talents God has given us?*

.007 surrender

- Why do you think honesty with God is so important?

- What do you think it means to truly surrender to God?

- In what ways is surrender a one-time event? In what ways is surrender an ongoing process?

- Do you think it's possible to surrender everything at once? Why or why not?

- Can you think of any areas of your life that still remain unsurrendered? If so, explain.

- What prevents you from fully surrendering to God? What steps can you take to overcome these obstacles?

- What area of your heart or life do you feel is currently being renovated by God?

holy reverberations

Read Matthew 11:28 and Hebrews 13:20–21.

- *What are some of the rewards of surrendering your life to Christ?*

- *Why do you think surrendering is so hard?*

- *What can you lose by surrendering yourself to Christ? What can you gain?*

.008 take care of my people

- In what ways has God challenged you to take care of his people? How are you taking care of his people right now?

- Why do you think God is so concerned with the poor?

- In what ways have you experienced poverty—whether it's relational, financial, personal, etc.?

- What has God been speaking to your heart regarding care for the poor and social injustices?

- Do you ever find that taking care of someone else actually helps you take care of yourself? If so, explain.

- Do you agree or disagree with the statement that "poverty comes in many different forms"? Explain.

- Why do you think God would speak two different directives to the Christians living on opposite sides of Lake Lanier?

holy reverberations

Read Leviticus 19:9–10.

- Why do you think God gave such specific direction regarding the edges of the harvest?

- In what specific ways can you incorporate "gleaning" in your modern life?

- Why do you think God is so concerned with the poor? What does his concern reveal about his character?

.009 bring them to me

- What is one of the toughest questions you've ever asked God?

- Does anything prevent you from asking God the toughest of questions? Explain.

- Margaret felt like God was comforting her when she heard, "This happens to some of my children." But God didn't leave her there. He invited her to bring the situation to him in prayer. Have you ever found yourself in a situation where the only thing you could do was pray? Describe.

- Are there any situations you've seen or found yourself in that you don't feel like you can bring to God? Explain.

- Why do you think people are afraid to ask God their most scandalous questions?

- Do you think there is a question that you could ask God that he has not heard before? Explain.

- When you think of the river in Revelation 22:1–2 that promises to "make glad the city of God" (Psalm 46:4), who do you look forward to seeing on its banks?

holy reverberations
Read Habakkuk 1:1–2:20.

- *What tough questions does Habakkuk ask God?*

- *How does God answer Habakkuk?*

- *How does the interaction of God and Habakkuk challenge your own prayer life?*

.010 you are not alone

- How do you respond when all you hear is silence from God?

- How do you tend to fill in the blanks in your own life when all you hear is silence?

- Why is isolation or the belief that you're the only one so dangerous?

- Why is the knowledge that you're not alone so life-giving?

- What's the toughest *Why* question you've ever asked God?

- What lines have you drawn in your own relationship with God?

- What steps do you need to take to erase the lines you've drawn with God?

holy reverberations

Read Luke 1:24–57.

- *What was unique about the pregnancies of Mary and Elizabeth?*

- *How do you think they were able to encourage each other in all the unusual events they were experiencing?*

- *Have you ever had someone in your life like Mary or Elizabeth during a difficult time? How were you able to encourage each other?*

awakened

- In what specific ways have you been immersed into the reality of God?

- What do you think God's voice sounds like? What adjectives would you use to describe God's voice?

- What has God been whispering to you?

- What sacred echoes have you recognized in your life while reading this book?

- What steps do you need to take to go from mere information to real transformation in your life?

- In what ways are you better able to recognize God's voice in your life?

holy reverberations

Read John 16:12–15 and 2 Timothy 3:16–17.

- *Why is it so important to listen to God's voice in our lives?*

- *What role does Scripture play in recognizing God's voice?*

- *What is the fruit of listening and obeying God's voice?*

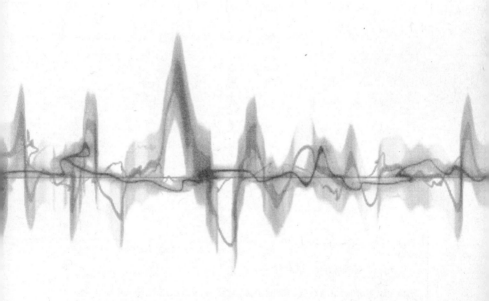

behind the scenes

exposed

Page 18: Now prayer is much more than asking God for things. It's a blend of thanksgiving, praise, and confession. Prayer can be outspoken or silent, a reflection of movement or stillness, an expression of sound or silence. Maybe that's why at the top of my prayer page I list adoration and praise first. This is my daily springboard into a river of prayer that ebbs and flows with gratefulness, repentance, confession, conversation, and too many questions to be tallied.

Page 19: Luke 18:1–8.

Page 21: 1 Kings 19:10.

Page 24: Acts 17:11.

Page 26: Leif is pronounced *Lay-f,* though all too often his name is mispronounced as *Leaf* or *Life.*

.001 i love you

Page 31: Yum. A sporty new word that can be found in the dictionary. I'll have to add the noun to my list which includes dandies like "carbage," the garbage that collects on the bottom of an automobile, and "floordrobe," the clothes that accumulate on the floor near your closet (not that I know about either one).

Page 31: *www.wm.edu/news/?id=4418* and *www.livescience.com/animals/061128_bat_faces.html*

Page 34: Deuteronomy 7:9; Psalm 36:7; Psalm 103:13; Proverbs 3:12;
Proverbs 8:17; Song of Solomon 2:4; John 3:16; John 13:34;
Romans 5:5; Romans 8:35–39; Ephesians 2:4–5; Ephesians 3:17–19;
1 John 4:7; 1 John 4:19.

Page 38: Hosea 1:2.

Page 39: Hosea 6:3.

Page 39: Mark 12:41–44.

Page 42: John 4:35 NIV.

.002 sing it again

Page 46: Revelation 4:8.

Page 46: Numbers 6:24–26.

Page 49: Isaiah 43:1–5.

Page 50: Genesis 4:3–7; Genesis 21:17; Acts 9:10–16. These encounters
were either God or an angel of God speaking.

Page 51: 1 Thessalonians 5:17.

Page 52: Luke 6:27.

.003 how long?

Page 60: Despite my contempt, frustration, and anger, God answered
that prayer eighteen months later in a small Episcopal church in
Steamboat Springs, Colorado.

Page 61: This is the first time the question is asked in the NASB, which
I use for personal study. Some other translations may pose the
question earlier due to the translation.

Page 62: Revelation 19:7–10.

Page 67: Matthew 3:17.

Page 67: Matthew 11:2–3.

Page 68: Matthew 11:4–6.

Page 68: Isaiah 29:18; Isaiah 35:6; the cleansing of lepers is implied in Isaiah 61:1; Isaiah 29:18; Implied in Isaiah 11:1–2; Isaiah 26:19; Isaiah 61:1–2.

Page 68: Isaiah 61:1–2.

Page 68: I discovered this teaching in a Jewish Commentary. David Stern, *Jewish New Testament Commentary* (Clarksville, Md.: Jewish New Testament Publications, 1999), 42.

Page 69: Psalm 40:1; Psalm 62:1–6; Isaiah 30:18; Isaiah 40:30–31.

Page 69: Isaiah 64:4.

.004 read it again

Page 72: As an author, pulling off a gotcha in a book is really fun! I'd love to know your response to this section. Email me at margaret@ margaretfeinberg.com.

Page 74: 2 Samuel 18:19–33.

Page 79: John 1:35–51.

Page 81: Matthew 7:9–11 (emphasis added).

Page 83: Ta 'anit 3:8; and see the Gemara on it at Ta 'anit 23a. David Stern, *Jewish New Testament Commentary* (Clarksville, Md.: Jewish New Testament Publications, 1999), 99.

Page 84: James 5:17–18.

.005 you follow me

Page 88: To date, I have quite a collection of these spiritual anchors. Passages like Isaiah 43, the story of creation in Genesis 1 and 2, and

the calling of the disciples in John 1 fasten me to the truth of who I
am and who I'm called to be.

Page 89: John 21:18–19.

.006 if you don't wear your crown

Page 105: Was this God or the adversary? One of the ways I can
often tell the difference is that while God brings conviction, the
adversary immerses his words with condemnation. Oddly, I didn't
feel conviction or condemnation, just a weightiness that much was
at stake. Over the next several weeks, I continued praying. Every few
days, the statement flashed back through my mind still with the same
burden. I often asked God if this echo was from him, and if so, what
did it mean?

Page 106: Matthew 27:29.

Page 107: Matthew 25:28.

Page 109: Gary Thomas, *The Beautiful Fight: Surrendering to the
Transforming Presence of God Every Day of Your Life* (Grand Rapids:
Zondervan), 133. Several years ago, I read *Experiencing God* by
Henry Blackaby. The book challenged readers to find what God was
doing and join him. I've never forgotten it.

Page 109: Revelation 4:11.

.007 surrender

Page 116: Matthew 8:22.

Page 120: Mark 10:29–30.

Page 121: In case you were wondering, he was not wearing all that gold
during the interview. And yes, for the record, he did say "I pity the
fool" during our time together.

Page 121: This story is powerfully retold in the film *End of the Spear*.

Page 122: Margaret Feinberg, "Steve Saint: In My Father's Footsteps," *New Man Magazine*, Sep/Oct 2001, *http://www.newmanmagazine.com/display.php?id=1343*

Page 122: Reading this, my friend Stan responded, "The sovereign God chose to create a universe in which responsible agents could make choices, and consequently in which sin/evil/pain/tragedy would be possible. Fellowship with automatons would not be fellowship at all. Sin, and all the consequences that flow from it, are the result of wrong creaturely choices, going back to the fall of Satan himself, and then to Adam and Eve. My faith in the goodness and love of God does not tolerate that he could himself have orchestrated or determined these events. But my faith in the goodness and sovereignty of God, and my own experience of such pain and evil, tells me that somehow in a mysterious way that I cannot really fathom at least in this life, God can and does take those poor and bad (yes, even evil) choices that his creatures make, and the pain and suffering endemic to this fallen world, and somehow bring good out of them, but without getting his own hands dirty. We see enough of that is this life, to have faith that this will ultimately and finally be true also."

.008 take care of my people

Page 132: vv.15–17.

Page 133: Revelation 3:17.

Page 135: James 1:27.

Page 139: Leviticus 19:9–10; Deuteronomy 14:28–29; Leviticus 19:13; Deuteronomy 15:12–15; Leviticus 25:39–42; Exodus 22:25; Deuteronomy 16:11–15.

Page 140: www.wcg.org/lit/bible/gospels/lukewealth.htm. "Open Letter to a Wealthy Man" by Michael Morrison opened my eyes to the teachings of finances in the gospel of Luke, and I am extremely grateful.

Page 140: Luke 18:22; 19:13–26; 19:2–10; 12:16–21; 15:13, 16:1; Luke 7:36–50; 10:35; 23:50–53; Luke 1:3.

Page 143: If God has been speaking to your heart concerning poverty, the poor, or social injustice, I'd love to hear what God has been echoing to you. Please email me at margaret@margaretfeinberg.com.

.009 bring them to me

Page 148: Mark 9:14–29.

Page 148: Mark 9:19.

Page 151: For a wonderful book on Jewish Midrash, check out *The Burning Word* by Judith M. Kunst (Brewster, Mass.: Paraclete, 2006).

Page 158: I think "somewhy" should be a word. Somehow, somewhere, and somewhat all got placement so let's add somewhy too!

Page 164: Revelation 22:1–2.

Page 165: Psalm 46:4–6; Genesis 2:9; 3:22, 24.

.010 you are not alone

Page 171: If you don't understand this lighthearted comment, simply find a friend who has IBS (irritable bowel syndrome) or anyone over the age of sixty. They will be happy to explain it to you.

Page 172: Proverbs 13:12.

Page 174: 1 Kings 19:4 .

Page 179: Genesis 18:14–15.

connection

A popular speaker at churches, colleges, women's retreats, and leading conferences such as Fusion, Catalyst, National Pastors Convention, and LeadNow, Margaret Feinberg invites people to discover the relevance of God and his Word in a modern world. Audiences love her ability to connect the practical with the spiritual.

Margaret currently lives in Morrison, Colorado, with her 6'8" husband, Leif. When she's not writing or traveling, she enjoys anything outdoors. She says some of her best moments are spent communicating with readers and leaders online.

**So if you want to put a smile on her face,
go ahead and drop her a line:**

Margaret Feinberg
PO Box 441
Morrison, Colorado 80465
Margaret@margaretfeinberg.com
www.margaretfeinberg.com
Facebook Tag: Margaret Feinberg
www.margaretfeinberg.blogspot.com
www.myspace.com/margaretfeinberg

friends

I wanted to introduce you to some of my friends. I know the people behind all of these organizations and I simply cannot rave enough about them. They are all making a difference in the world in significant ways and beautifully represent the diverse things God is doing in this generation. When it comes to leaving the world a better place, I believe in three things: Give Voice. Give Time. Give Money. We support all the friends listed here in those ways and encourage you to join in the fun!

"Come, Let's Dance" supports orphans, abandoned street kids, and the destitute in Uganda by empowering future leaders, community development, and sustainable projects.

www.comeletsdance.org

JustOne is a non-profit organization that was formed to stimulate greater global awareness about extreme poverty, and to provoke compassionate ideas and intelligent giving in order to provide sustainable relief. We are a collective voice for the victims of social injustice—the one(s) living in geographical and situational poverty; the one(s) orphaned through death, disease, and desertion; the one(s) trafficked into slavery throughout the world.

www.just4one.org

The RightNow Campaign is a movement of twenty- and thirty-somethings trading in the pursuit of the American Dream for a world that desperately needs Christ. We connect our generation and their passions, skills, and desires to actual opportunities to put their faith in action.

Check out www.rightnow.org

16.9 FL OZ (500 ML)

Evotional.com is the daily blog of Mark Batterson, lead pastor of National Community Church in Washington, DC and author of *Wild Goose Chase*. Through his blog, Mark shares his insights on life and leadership.

www.evotional.com

Fermi Project educates Christians about their unique role and responsibility in culture. The *Fermi Words* digital magazine is a hybrid of written and spoken words created to provoke conversations.

For an annual contribution of $59, subscribers receive filtered, synthesized, and compressed ideas monthly through commissioned essays and eighteen-minute audio and video presentations.

www.fermiproject.com

JUNKY CAR CLUB
LIVING WITH LESS SO WE CAN GIVE MORE

The Junky Car Club is an official car club whose members are learning to live with less so they can give more. The JCC is filled with happy drivers who are politely rebelling against consumerism and have made a lifestyle choice to drive beaters, clunkers, and junkers. Our members then use their dough to support social justice organizations and sponsor children in poverty through Compassion International.

Membership is FREE and you can join the club at www.JunkyCarClub.com

Cross Bar X exists to reach urban and rural youth with the gospel of Jesus Christ. We want everything we do to point to Christ, whether it is eating breakfast or whitewater rafting. Our desire is to see every camper form and deepen their relationship with Jesus Christ.

www.crossbarxcamp.org

bottomless thanks to ...

Brilliant theologian Craig Blomberg (no pressure, promise)

Fellow grasshopper Jonathan Merritt

Partner-in-crime Dave Terpstra

Ever encouraging Ven Taylor

Fan club president Carolyn Haggard

Favorite fashionista Carly Barron

My dear Angela Scheff

BFF and twin Amena Brown

BFFF Janella Griggs

Superhero Dave Zimmerman

Hopeful, hope-filling Mark Rice

Generous Natalie Gillespie

Thought-provoking Trevor Bron

Inspiring Lori and Jason Boucher

Fantastic Chris and Christy Ferebee

Wise Stan Gundry

Blogging buddy Rick Stilwell

My forever love Leif

the
organic
God

margaret feinberg

.001 an organic appetite

It was one thing for my Jewish father to marry my non-Jewish mother. It was another thing completely for both of them to become Christians within a month of each other eight years into their marriage. Let's just say that the decision did not go down too well with the Jewish side of the family. (Imagine *My Big Fat Greek Wedding* without the happy ending.) A month after their conversion, I was conceived, and less than a year after my parents became Christians, I was welcomed into a world of religious tension. I didn't know it at the time, but I became the bundle of glue that held the family together, because as upset as my Jewish grandmother was at my father, she wasn't going to give up access to her only grandchild.

As a result of my parents' backgrounds, I was raised in a Christian home with hues of Judaism. Think matza ball soup at Christmastime. I never knew how many gifts my Jewish grandmother was going to give—whether I would hit the jackpot with the stack-o-gifts that accompanies Hanukkah, or receive the one big present that inadvertently acknowledged Christmas even though it was still wrapped in Hanukkah paper. The confusion ended when Grandma began giving the gift that embraced the fullness of my Jewish heritage: a check.

Throughout the years, I managed to learn a few random words in Yiddish, develop a quirky Jewish sense of humor, and inherit an undeniable sense of chutzpah. I developed a desire to know how these worlds that seemed so opposed in my childhood could ever get along. I also developed a hunger to know God. This hunger wasn't anything I conjured up but rather seemed to be part of the "me-package," like a strand of DNA, though it took years to fully manifest itself. My initial interaction with Scripture wasn't so much out of longing as it was out of desperation. I was having terrible nightmares—the kind you can't forget even when you're an adult.

On a sunny, breeze-softened afternoon, I was fishing alongside a creek in a forest filled with maple and oak trees. Sitting on the moss-carpeted shore, I held a thin wooden fishing pole. I felt a slight tug on the line and an unmistakable surge of excitement. I began pulling back on the pole. It arched at the weight of the catch. Without warning, a huge shark with beady eyes and enormous yellow razor-sharp teeth came out of the water and toward my face.

I awoke, breathless. Heart pounding. Body covered in sweat. I knew sharks didn't jump out of creeks and eat people, but now I wasn't so sure. I didn't want to fall back asleep ever again. Would the next nightmare be worse?

These night terrors continued for months. My parents held me. Prayed for me. Comforted me when they heard my screams. But the dreams didn't stop until I made a personal discovery. Somehow, I figured out that if I read the Bible before I went to bed, I would sleep soundly. It's a strange equation:

Bible before bed = No nightmares

The concept made perfect sense when I was eight. I couldn't explain why it worked, I just knew that it did. And when you're facing man-eating sharks, you'll do whatever it takes to make them go away.

Two-plus decades later, I'm sometimes tempted to shrug off my miracle cure as an oddity or merely chance, except for the fact that those evening readings made God all the more real and personal. I'm humbled that God would so tenderly and intimately embrace a child with simple faith. And I am staggered to realize how God was preparing me, even then, to know him better.

Somewhere along the way, reading the Bible actually became enjoyable and not just a cure for nightmares. The stories of kings and queens and prophets and pilgrims came alive, and of course, the Jesus-man captured my heart as well as my imagination. What did he look like? What did his voice sound like? What did his hands feel like? I wanted to know.

Now there were a few years when I forgot about my experience as a young girl. I tried to run away from God and en-gaged in an extracurricular activity better known as partying like a rock star. I kissed too many boys and drank too much beer and enjoyed a thoroughly hollow good time, but deep down inside, I knew that partying wasn't the life for me. I returned to the routine I had learned at eight years old and began reading my Bible again.

More than a decade later, I still want to know God. The desire hasn't cooled. At times I have allowed myself to be overpow-ered by other desires. Busyness. Lesser loves. Laziness. And the temptation to let someone else do all the hard work of digging into the rich reservoirs of Scripture.

All too often I find myself tempted to live a distracted life. You know the kind—the one where, within the busyness of life, you still manage to perform the stand-up, sit-down, clap, clap, clap of regular church attendance; drop a check in the offering plate; hope for a new nugget of knowledge, understanding, or insight in the weekly sermon; and check off a random, albeit short, list of acts of kindness to others. Somehow I'm sup-posed to feel like I'm living the Jesus-driven life.

I don't.

That's when the hunger appears in my belly and overtakes my soul, grumbling that there must be more. Even in the mun-dane, I find myself wanting more of God. Surely I'm not the only person who lies in bed at night wondering, *Is this all there is?* I can't be the only one who looks at the seemingly rich buffet of everything this world has to offer and loses my appetite, because even with countless provisions, friends, and activities—many of which are not only good but could be classified as godly—I can't shake this sense that there's more.

The hunger growls that there's more of God not only to uncover but to discover.

The hunger cries out that there's more of this God-infused life to live.

The hunger reminds me that there's more.

I want to go there. But how do I find the way?

When I reflect on my life map so far, I realize that spiritual hunger, the enablement to love and long for a relationship with our Creator, is not just God's greatest command—it is also his greatest gift. It's the kind of desire that compelled the psalmist not only to ask, "Whom have I in heaven but you?" but to answer, "Earth has nothing I desire besides you."

That's why I began praying for spiritual hunger and haven't stopped. As my prayers funnel toward heaven, I can't help but reflect on my own spiritual journey and wonder how much of God I really know and how much of God I simply take other people's word for or dismiss altogether. If God is bighearted, then why am I tempted to live with a closed hand? If God is surprisingly talkative, then why don't I take more time to listen? If God is deeply mysterious, then why do I sometimes lose the intrigue?

In the quietness of my own soul, I cannot help but wonder, *How much of God do I really know?*

If we met on the street, would I even recognize him?

In the humility of honesty and a soul laid bare: I do not know.

Such realizations shake the core of who I am. I'm pointedly reminded of the day an older woman I barely knew asked if my mother was Jewish when she heard my last name.

"No, just my father," I explained.

"Well, then you're not Jewish," she replied. "To be Jewish, your mom must be Jewish."

I was taken aback. I had a Jewish father, a Jewish grandmother who escaped Poland at the onset of World War II, and I knew how to make a mean bowl of matza ball soup. Even my best friend was Jewish. What more did you have to do to be a half-Jew?

It turned out that the nosy woman was right. Orthodox Judaism embraces matrilineal descent, or the belief that a child's Jewish identity is passed down through the mother.

Only recently has the reformed movement within Judaism embraced patrilineal descent. Regardless, they still require that the child be raised Jewish—which I was not. .

The incident left me feeling like a spiritual bastard child. Once the paralyzing effect of the conversation wore off and my mom assured me that I was my father's daughter, I grew an even deeper desire to understand how these two worlds—that of Jewish descent and Christian upbringing—intersect. It also left me hungrier for God. What does it mean to be his child? How does that affect my identity, my behavior, the very core of who I am? I knew he was the only one who could offer any resolve.

Deep down inside I still hunger for a true, pure relationship with the Organic God—the One True God. The God of Abraham, Isaac, and Jacob. In him is found the mysterious wonder of the Trinity. He is Father, Son, and Holy Spirit—one luminous essence in whom there is no shadow of change, stirred by the eternal and dynamic relationship of the three persons who live and love completely free of any need or self-interest.

Why describe God as organic? More and more I realize that my own understanding of God is largely polluted. I have preconceived notions, thoughts, and biases when it comes to

God. I have a tendency to favor certain portions of Scripture over others. I have a bad habit of reading some stories with a been-there-done-that attitude, knowing the end of the story before it begins, and in the process denying God's ability to speak to me through it once again.

If that weren't enough, more often than not, I find myself compartmentalizing God. He is more welcome in some areas of my life than others. Prayer, Bible study, Scripture memorization, journaling, and other spiritual disciplines become like items to be checked off a to-do list that is eventually crumpled up and thrown away rather than savored and reflected upon. The result is that my understanding and perception of God is clouded, much like the dingy haze of pollution that hangs over most major cities. The person in the middle of a city looking up at the sky doesn't always realize just how much their view and perceptions are altered by the smog. Without symptoms such as burning eyes or an official warning of scientists or media, no one may even notice just how bad the pollution has become.

That's why I describe God as organic. While it's a word usually associated with food grown without chemical-based fertilizers or pesticides, *organic* is also used to describe a lifestyle: simple, healthful, and close to nature. Those are all things I desire in my relationship with God. I hunger for the simplicity. I want to approach God in childlike faith, wonder, and awe. I long for more than just spiritual life but spiritual health—whereby my soul is not just renewed and restored but becomes a source of refreshment for others. And I want to be close to nature, not mountain ridges and shorelines as much as God's nature working in and through me. Such a God-infused lifestyle requires me to step away from any insta-grow shortcuts and dig deep into the soil of spiritual formation found only in God.

Natural. Pure. Essential.

I want to discover God again, anew, in a fresh way. I want my love for him to come alive again so that my heart dances at the very thought of him. I want a real relationship with him—a relationship that isn't altered by perfumes, additives, chemicals, or artificial flavors that promise to make it sweeter, sourer, or tastier than it really is. I want to know a God who in all his fullness would allow me to know him. I want a relationship that is real, authentic, and life-giving even when it hurts. I want to know God stripped of as many false perceptions as possible. Such a journey risks exposure, honesty, and even pain, but I'm hungry and desperate enough to go there. I want to know the Organic God.

I have this hunch that when God grants us a whim or a whiff of a desire to know him, we should take action—and fast—because those windows of opportunity may pass, and we may once again become satisfied with the smorgasbord of this world, rather than the world to come. I knew I had to do something, but what?

I decided once again to read the book that God gave me. You probably have a copy too. Usually when I give a book to someone, I want to build a relationship—to develop conversation, share ideas, and grow together. The gift of a book is a tangible effort to take the relationship to a new intensity—so it becomes deeper, richer, and broader than ever before.

Recognizing that you cannot love that which you do not know and experience, I began my journey to know God more by going through key books of the Old Testament and the entire New Testament, recording every verse that described a characteristic or attribute of God. As you can imagine, I've filled dozens and dozens of pages. Along the way, I found unimaginably breathtaking aspects of God.

In some regards, the journey to know God isn't too different from a first encounter with someone you've never met. I want to know what God looks like and what his interests are. I want to know his likes and dislikes. I want to know what makes him tick and also what ticks him off. I want to fall in love all over again. I want to know God.

Through the Scripture, God invites us to discover the wonders of Jesus shining in its pages. But it takes work. Like peeling an orange, reading the Bible sometimes feels messy and sticky and time-consuming. But once you bite into its pulpy juiciness—oh, how its flavors dance on the taste buds.

And while we relish the taste, the nutrients also feed our soul. With the Spirit's enzymes, we unknowingly, automatically, miraculously digest the words on the page, until they transform our actions and even our attitudes. Indeed, the book God gives us is like no other. God seems far more concerned with transformation than mere information. If you look real close, you'll notice that scrawled on every page is an invitation to know the author.

The truth is—God glows. His glory illuminates the heavens. Jesus, by his very nature, is brilliance. The One described as the light of the world does not contain a shadow of darkness. And the Holy Spirit ushers the spiritual dawn into our lives. Like the fireflies of the sea that beckon our imaginations to another world, the truth of God invites us to embrace the fullness of the life we were meant to live. As we look to him, we can't help but become more radiant.

The vastness. The beauty. The power. The splendor. The glory.

It looks like luminescence is already beginning to surface.

.001 An Organic Appetite

Page 228: Psalm 73:25. One of the greatest desires or hungers that I see of men and women in both the Old and New Testaments is to know God. Moses bravely asks God, "If you are pleased with me, teach me your ways so I may know you and continue to find favor with you" (Exodus 33:13). The psalmist's heart cry reverberates with a desire to know God and his ways—"Show me your ways, O Lord, teach me your paths; guide me in your truth and teach me, for you are God my Savior, and my hope is in you all day long" (Psalm 25:4–5).

Page 233: If you don't have a copy of the Bible, please email me at *margaret@margaretfeinberg.com*, and I'll make sure one is sent to you.

Page 234: The Book of Common Prayer provides one of the best summaries of drinking from the rich wells of Scripture: "Read, mark, learn and inwardly digest."

The Organic God

Margaret Feinberg

Imagine what it would look like to have an organic relationship with God — one that is stripped of all pollutants and additives of this world.

The Organic God removes the unhealthy fillers and purifies our relationship with the God of the Scriptures.

Through personal stories and scriptural insights, Margaret Feinberg shares glimpses of God's character — bighearted, kind, beautiful, mysterious — that point you to an authentic and naturally spiritual relationship with him, allowing you to truly discover God in a healthy, refreshing new way. You won't be able to help but fall in love all over again.

Hardcover, Printed 978-0-310-27244-1

Pick up a copy today at your favorite bookstore!

Audio Downloads

The Organic God

Margaret Feinberg

Audio Download,
Unabridged 978-0-310-30498-2

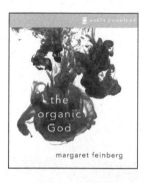

The Sacred Echo

Margaret Feinberg

Audio Download,
Unabridged 978-0-310-30268-1

Pick up a copy today at your favorite retail outlet!

For a list of Margaret's speaking engagements, please visit
www.margaretfeinberg.com